# HOW TO
# REALLY *SELL*
# YOUR HOUSE

**A Consumer's Guide to Estate Agency**

# HOW TO REALLY *SELL* YOUR HOUSE

A Consumer's Guide to Estate Agency

## Adam Walker

Beaumont Publications

Published by

**Beaumont Publications**
**Beaumont House**
**Nottingham Road**
**Heronsgate**
**Herts**
**WD3 5DP**

ISBN 0 9529023 0 3

Typeset by Harding House
37 Parkfield Chorleywood Herts WD3 5AZ

Produced for Beaumont Publications by
Chase Production Services Chipping Norton

# CONTENTS

## Section 1    Choosing the Right Estate Agent

## Section 2    Finding a Buyer

## Section 3    Getting the Sale Through to Completion

# PREFACE

A great many 'How to sell your house' books have been published during the last fifteen years. Some cover the financial aspects of a move such as raising a mortgage, some cover the legal side of the transaction and some cover how to sell without using an estate agent. However, during the whole of the time that I have been associated with the property market I have never come across a book that explained how to choose and get the best out of an estate agent.

This struck me as very strange. Most house sellers sell through an estate agent and yet there was no such thing as a consumer's guide to estate agency. I felt that there should be and decided to write a book that would answer some of the many questions that I have been asked as a consultant during the last fifteen years.

The finished book is in three parts. The first section covers how to choose the right estate agent. Ideally this section should be read about eight weeks before the property is put onto the market. The second section explains how a good agent should go about finding a buyer. This section should be read as soon as the property is put onto the market. The final section explains some of the common sales progressing problems and gives advice on how to overcome them. This section should be used as a reference section to dip into as and when a problem occurs.

This book would not have been possible without the help of a great many people. In particular I should like to thank; Black Horse Agencies, Palmer Snell, the Woolwich Building Society and the Royal Institute of Chartered Surveyors, all of which provided statistical and other information for use in the appendices.

I should also like to thank my secretary Lyn Harding for her patience, good humour and attention to detail during the many drafts of the book and Chase Production Services for their work on the production side.

**In this book please read he to mean he or she.**

# SECTION 1

# CHOOSING THE RIGHT ESTATE AGENT

# 1

# DO I REALLY NEED AN ESTATE AGENT AT ALL?

More than three-quarters of all house sellers use an estate agent. They do so because they believe that, even after allowing for commission, an agent will achieve a higher price for their property than they could achieve themselves. They are usually right.

## WHY WILL AN ESTATE AGENT ACHIEVE A HIGHER PRICE?

The price that is achieved for a property is determined, largely, by the law of supply and demand. If a property is exposed to a greater number of potential buyers, it will usually sell for a higher price.

One of the most important functions of an estate agent is, therefore, to act as an efficient net to catch every potential house buyer in the price range. When it comes to finding potential buyers, an estate agent has four important advantages over the private seller. They are:

### Newspaper advertising

An estate agent will run prominent advertisements in the local newspapers each week. The number of enquiries generated is related very closely to the size of the advertisement. A small private advertisement would do well to generate half a dozen enquiries. The estate agent's full page advertisement will generate many times this many.

A second point to consider regarding advertising is that many potential purchasers, particularly those from out of the area, buy a local newspaper only once. Having registered with all the local agents, they then wait to be contacted with details of suitable properties. By advertising for only one week the private vendor will reach only a fraction of these buyers.

### High street premises

Many buyers like to register by calling into the estate agent's office in person. Out-of-town buyers in particular, tend to find 'estate agents' row' and register with all the agents in it. The lack of high street premises will further reduce the number of potential purchasers that the private vendor is able to attract.

### *Yellow Pages*

Many buyers register with agents by working through *Yellow Pages*. The lack of an entry here will further hamper the private vendor.

### For Sale boards

The typical estate agent will have several dozen For Sale boards up at any one time. Each one of these boards will attract several new buyers and cumulatively they will be responsible for attracting around a quarter of all buyers. The private vendor with just his own single For Sale will fail to attract most of these purchasers.

Given all these advantages, an estate agent should be able to attract many times more purchasers for a property than a private vendor. Consequently, even a bad agent will usually be able to achieve a better price for your property than you could yourself.

## OTHER BENEFITS OF USING AN AGENT

In addition to finding the maximum number of potential purchasers, a good estate agent will be able to help with your sale in several other important ways. These include:

- **Valuation advice** A good agent will give advice on the value of your property and help you to decide on the optimum asking price.

- **Marketing** A good agent will play an active role in persuading potential purchasers to view your property.

- **Security** A good agent will check out potential viewers to ensure that they are genuine.

- **Negotiation** A good agent will use his negotiation skills to obtain the highest possible price.

- **Qualification** A good agent will check out your prospective buyers to ensure that they are actually in a position to proceed with the transaction.

- **Supervision** A good agent will keep a close eye on your sale and help to resolve any problems that arise prior to completion.

It is certainly possible to sell a house privately but there is no doubt that a good agent will earn his fee many times over. I would urge you to use one.

# 2

# HOW TO CHOOSE THE RIGHT ESTATE AGENT

In most large towns there is a bewildering selection of estate agents to choose from. To the casual observer they might appear to be all very much the same. On closer examination you will find that they most certainly are not. The best agent in the town might be able to achieve thousands of pounds more for your property than his least effective competitor. With this sort of money at stake it is worth going to considerable trouble to choose the right agent for the job.

The tell-tale signs that differentiate an outstanding agent from an average one can be grouped under two categories: the 'marketing campaign' and the 'service standards'.

## THE MARKETING CAMPAIGN

The number of potential purchasers that each agent has on his books will be governed by the effectiveness of his marketing campaign. The most effective agent could have three or four times more buyers on his register than his least effective competitor and this gives him a much better chance of achieving a premium price for your property. The effectiveness of each agent's marketing campaign can be judged by looking at the three key areas of advertising, board presence and office position.

### Newspaper advertising

Newspaper advertising is the single most important source of potential purchasers and it is, therefore, worth taking some trouble to assess each agent's effectiveness in this area. Collect together all the local newspapers for a three to four week period and look for the following features:

- **Size** The leading agents will nearly always have the largest advertisements. There is a direct correlation between the size of the advertisement and the number of enquiries generated.

- **Choice of publication** Advertising costs vary widely between different newspapers and, generally speaking, advertisers get what they pay for. If in doubt you might consider phoning the local newspapers to enquire about advertising rates and circulation figures so that you can make your own assessment of which agent has the highest local advertising budget.

- **Position** Certain pages in a newspaper generate far more enquiries than others. Generally speaking:

  - The nearer the front the better

  - Right hand pages are better than left hand pages

  - The front cover, back cover and centre pages usually get a good response

  The leading agents usually book the prime positions on a long term contract. You should be cautious about using an agent who has a consistently poor position.

- **Frequency** The leading agents will advertise every week throughout the year (with the possible exception of December). You should be cautious about using an agent who advertises only sporadically.

- **Layout** The advertisement should be easy to read with an attractive layout and plenty of space between the properties. Advertisements that cram too many properties into a small space generate fewer enquiries.

- **Colour** Full colour advertisements generate far more enquiries than black and white ones. If only two or three agents are advertising in colour, they will have a considerable advantage over their competitors.

- **Variety** Beware of the agent who advertises the same houses every week– he may be having trouble attracting new instructions (and there is usually a reason for this).

- **Content** What sort of properties are advertised by each agent? Are they cheaper or more expensive than your own? There is no point putting an ordinary house with an up-market agent or vice versa.

## Board presence

Estate agents' boards are another very important source of enquiries. Do a rough count of which agents have the largest number of boards up in your area. It is likely that each of these boards will have already generated several enquiries from potential purchasers for your property. Pay particular attention to Sold boards. The agent who has recently sold several houses in your road could well be the best agent to handle the sale of your house.

## Office position

A large percentage of potential purchasers like to register their requirements in person. The position and prominence of an estate agent's office is often, therefore, an important factor. The prominent High Street office will usually register several times as many potential purchasers as its small backstreet competitor.

## STANDARDS OF CUSTOMER SERVICE

Before you rush off to instruct the agent with the biggest advertisement and the most prominent office, you should pause to consider that registering the largest number of potential purchasers is not an automatic guarantee of success. In order to sell houses effectively, an agent needs to persuade potential purchasers to view the properties that they have for sale. It is here that so many agents fall down.

There is only one way to establish which of the local agents offers the best standard of service and that is to register with them all as a buyer. If you are moving locally you can register as a genuine purchaser. If you are not buying locally you could register as a purchaser for a property that is similar to the one which you wish to sell, perhaps saying that your present property is rented. You will find that the level of service which you receive as a purchaser varies enormously between agents. The signs of an effective agent are:

- **Initial response**  The telephone should be answered promptly and cheerfully.

- **Rapport**  The agent should work hard to build a rapport rather than just reading questions off a list.

- **Qualification**  The agent should establish quickly whether you are in a position to buy immediately or whether you have a property yet to sell. This will enable him to work more effectively by spending more time with his best prospects.

- **Sales effort** The agent should describe a couple of suitable properties over the phone and ask you for an immediate commitment to view them. This is far more effective than just passively sending out details.

- **Property details** An accurately chosen selection of property details should arrive by post the next working day. Some firms might even deliver details by hand to local purchasers. The details should be attractively presented, preferably with full colour photographs.

- **Telephone follow-up** The effective agent will telephone you approximately 24 hours after you have received the details and make another attempt to get a viewing appointment. Purchasers who are followed up by telephone are far more likely to view than those who are left to contact the agent themselves.

- **Ongoing follow-up** The effective agent will continue to telephone you at least once a week to try to persuade you to view properties that are new to the market.

- **Persistence** To be effective an agent must be persistent. You need someone who will really *sell* your property, not just wait for someone to buy it. However, the effective agent should know when to give up gracefully and should never become over-aggressive.

You will usually find that the service given by one or two agents stands head and shoulders above the service given by the rest. These agents should definitely be included on your short list.

### Owning up

It is unlikely that you will ever need to own up to your subterfuge. You can tell the agents that did not measure up that you have now found a property to buy. The agents that you do choose to invite to value your property will often not notice that someone on their applicant register has asked for a valuation appointment. If they do, you can simply admit that you wanted to test their service before instructing them. They will probably be quite flattered to have been chosen by such an objective process.

### HOW NOT TO CHOOSE AN ESTATE AGENT

As a home owner you are likely to receive regular approaches from agents who are touting for business. These will come in a number of formats:

**The printed leaflet**  A typical message would be 'Now is the time to sell. Call Bloggs estate agents for a free valuation without obligation.' Many estate agents deliver tens of thousands of such leaflets every year. The fact that you have received one does not mean that the company who sent it will be any better able to sell your house than the others.

**The photocopied letter** A typical message would be 'Dear Householder, We have just sold a house in your road and urgently need similar properties in the area.' This type of letter deserves to be taken a little more seriously. The agent would not have chosen your road if he did not have a demand for houses in it. However, if you do respond to such an approach you should ask for the agent to prove that he really has sold a property and that he has other buyers available for similar properties in the area.

**The individually addressed letter** The format of this letter will be similar to the photocopied letter described above and it should be dealt with in a similar way. The fact that it is addressed to you by name means only that the agent has looked up your name on the electoral register, which is available in the public library.

Although it may sometimes be worth responding to a touting letter, you should not allow the receipt of one to influence unduly your choice of agent. You are far more likely to find the right agent to market your property by objective research than by responding to a cleverly written letter.

## SELECTING THE FINAL SHORT LIST

Having finished your study of all the local agents you will be in a position to compile a short list of agents that you wish to see. Sometimes one agent will win hands down in every category, but more often than not you will be forced to compromise. Perhaps the agent with the biggest advertisement and the most prominent office gave you very poor services as a buyer. This could be a business that is in decline. Perhaps the dynamic manager who built the office up has recently been replaced by someone of a lower calibre. Whatever the reason, such a company is best avoided. At the other end of the scale you may have received outstanding service from an agent with a backstreet office and sporadic advertising. Again you should be cautious. Service is important but it cannot make up for a lack of potential buyers to sell to.

The safest choice would be to confine your list to companies who score reasonably well in both the key areas of effective marketing and effective customer service. On this basis you should select three or four agents to value your property.

# 3

# HOW MUCH IS MY PROPERTY WORTH?

## THE IMPORTANCE OF THOROUGH RESEARCH

Before you invite an estate agent to value your property you must first establish what it is worth. This may seem like a contradiction in terms but the fact is that estate agents' valuations are often inaccurate. This can happen for a number of reasons.

- **Deliberate overvaluation** Some estate agents give deliberately over-optimistic valuations because they know that it will help them to get more properties onto their books.

- **Poor research** An estate agent should have up-to-date knowledge about the prices achieved for other properties in the area that have recently sold. Poor research is a very common reason for an inaccurate valuation.

- **Inexperience** Too many firms of estate agents send staff out on valuation appointments who do not have sufficient experience to value accurately.

- **Local knowledge** Even an experienced estate agent will not be able to value a property accurately until he has been working in the local area for several months.

The only way to protect yourself against the consequences of an inaccurate valuation is to undertake the most comprehensive price research on your own behalf. In some countries the actual selling price achieved in every property transaction is a matter of public record. In the UK this information often is not publicly available and a degree of subterfuge may be required to obtain the necessary background information.

If you have not already done so, you should reconsider the idea of registering with some of the local agents as a buyer in order to obtain a selection of sales particulars of properties that are similar to your own. If you really do not wish to undertake this type of research, an alternative would be to look through back issues of the local property newspaper to find similar properties (back issues of the local papers are available from the library). The more properties you can find, the more likely it is that your personal valuation will be accurate.

## USING THE INFORMATION

The value of a property is determined by two factors: the prices achieved for similar properties that have recently been sold, and the asking prices of properties that are currently on the market and are competing for the same buyers as your own.

It is relatively easy to establish the value of a house in a road when there are other similar properties. The typical process would be:

Step 1     Research the asking prices of the last five or six properties in the road that have been offered for sale.

Step 2     Ignore properties which were markedly cheaper or more expensive than the others (there is always a reason).

Step 3     Average the price of the remaining properties.

Step 4     Deduct 5% from the final price to allow for the average difference between the asking and selling prices.

## VALUING A MORE INDIVIDUAL PROPERTY

If you own a more individual property you will need to apply a number of adjustment factors to the comparable properties that are available. Some of the most important factors to take into account are:

■ **Extensions and improvements** You will not generally recover the full cost of extensions and improvements. The proportion of the original cost that is recovered will depend upon the nature of the improvement, for example:

High cost recovery (up to 100%)
• Addition of extra bedroom in a style that is in keeping with the original property
• Addition of central heating
• Redecoration in a neutral style
• Addition of a garage

Medium cost recovery (up to 50%)
- Addition of ground floor-flat roofed extension
- Addition of conservatory
- Fitted Kitchen
- Modernisation of bathroom
- Loft conversion

Low cost recovery (less than 25%)
- Addition of outdoor swimming pool
- Addition of ground floor bathroom
- Double glazing
- Cavity wall insulation

Some improvements can substantially reduce the value of the property, for example:
- Extensions that occupy the entire garden
- Stone Cladding
- Double glazing on period property
- Removal of period features (Fireplaces, decorative plasterwork, etc.)

■ **Repairs** As with improvements, you are unlikely to recover the full cost of repairs that have been made to a property. Most buyers underestimate the cost of repairs and some are prepared to pay a premium for a house in poor condition in order to have the satisfaction of refurbishing it in their own taste.

■ **Area** In many towns a house in one road can command a very substantial premium over houses in the next. It is impossible to generalise about this but the boundaries are usually well-known locally.

■ **Location** A house on a busy road, or one backing onto a railway line will be worth substantially less than an identical house in a quiet street nearby. An extremely adverse location could reduce the value of a property by up to half.

■ **New developments** Many people will pay a premium to live in a brand new house. All new properties must therefore be excluded from your comparable evidence.

## CHECKING THE ACCURACY OF YOUR VALUATION

You can check the accuracy of your personal valuation by cross referencing it in a number of ways.

### How much did you pay?

Your local library will be able to provide you with a table showing the average rise in property values for each year since you purchased your property. Add the appropriate percentage increase to the price which you originally paid for your property. How does it compare to your own valuation?

### Current value of properties which you rejected as a purchaser

Before you bought your present property, you will almost certainly have viewed and rejected a number of alternative properties. Check to see if any of these properties, or others that are similar to them, are currently on the market. How does the asking price of each of these properties compare to your own valuation?

### Remortgage valuations

If you have remortgaged your house at any time, try adding the average percentage rise in property values since the remortgage to the surveyor's valuation. How does this figure compare to your own valuation?

### Friends and acquaintances who have recently bought and sold

People are strangely reticent about revealing the price that they paid or obtained for their property but there is no harm in asking. People often tell their neighbours that they paid more or less for their property than they really did. You should therefore treat all information obtained in this way with the greatest suspicion, particularly information which is passed on by a third party.

Once you have done everything possible to research and check the accuracy of your personal valuation you are ready to begin to prepare for the estate agents' valuation appointments.

# 4

# PREPARING YOUR PROPERTY FOR SALE

## PRESENTATION IS VITAL

The maxim 'presentation is vital' was never more true than when selling a house. It is therefore extremely important to carry out any necessary cosmetic work before you put your property on the market.

House Buyers form their impressions very quickly – indeed research shows that half of all buyers make the final decision before they even get inside the front door! If such a high proportion of buyers are going to make their decision from outside then this is where you too must start.

Go and stand in the street at least a hundred yards away from your property. Take a good hard look and try to see it through the eyes of someone who has never seen it before. What do you see? Have the neighbours' houses been decorated more recently than yours? If so consider redecorating at least the front elevation.

Move slowly forwards, ten yards at a time. What do you see as you move closer? Could your teenage son be persuaded to park his battered old car somewhere else for a few weeks? Are any tiles missing from the roof? Does the hedge need trimming? Is the front fence in good condition? Does the front garden need tidying?

Enter the front garden. Does the gate operate smoothly? Is the front door in good decorative condition? Are there cobwebs in the porch? Does the door bell work?

Open the front door and step inside. Take a long critical look at the entrance hall. Bear in mind that it is the first room that potential purchasers will see and consider whether any work is necessary to brighten it up. Before you leave the entrance hall think carefully about what order the rooms in the house should be shown in. It is important to ensure that buyers see the most attractive rooms first.

Go round the house in the order that purchasers will see it and check each room thoroughly. In particular look for the following:

- Does any room need redecorating?
- Are there any stains or damp patches?
- Are there any cracks?
- Do the carpets need cleaning?
- Do any light bulbs need replacing?
- Are any windows overshadowed by trees or foliage?
- Are the windows dirty?
- Is the garden tidy?
- Are the fences in good order?

**Decorating to sell** If any room does need redecorating it is best to stick to light neutral colours which will make the room look bigger and lighter. Save expressing your individualism for your next house.

**More extensive works** Generally speaking it is not worth undertaking more major works in order to facilitate a sale. If you are thinking of undertaking repair work, you should bear in mind that most purchasers tend to underestimate the true cost of repairs so you are likely to be better off by leaving them as they are. If you are thinking of undertaking cosmetic work you should bear in mind that most buyers would prefer to buy a cheaper property and install their own choice of kitchen, bathroom or carpets, etc.

### Finishing touches

In addition to the above you might also consider:

- **Net curtains** Net curtains block out a great deal of natural light and can also make rooms look smaller. Consider taking them down whilst the house is on the market.

- **Curtains** Rooms can be made to seem very dark by heavy curtains which cannot be drawn back off the windows. Consider tying such curtains back whilst the house is on the market.

- **Furniture** Large pieces of furniture will make rooms seem smaller. Consider repositioning or even storing such items whilst the house is on the market.

- **Flowers** A hanging basket in the porch or fresh flowers in the entrance hall can make a real difference to a buyer's first impression of your house.

When considering all of the above, bear in mind the golden rule that 'the sooner they see it the more important it is'. A dingy entrance hall could be extremely off-putting; your daughter's fluorescent purple fourth bedroom will have less effect on a potential purchaser's decision.

## Organise a trial viewing

Once you have attended to all the necessary jobs, ask a friend to 'view' your property. Ask them to point out anything that you have missed. Ask them also for their honest opinion on one very important matter. How does your house smell? I am not joking. Despite the fact that smell is one of our most powerful senses, many people do not realise that the human nose is only programmed to detect new smells. To you Fido stopped 'smelling' when he was a 12-week-old puppy. To strangers he could now smell strongly enough to prevent a sale for months! Even the bravest estate agent will not tell you this – find a friend who will.

## Consider paying for a surveyor's report

Very few people consider instructing a surveyor to look at a house that they are selling, but a survey report can be a valuable marketing tool. Many buyers are nervous about making an offer for a house for fear that problems will later be revealed on survey. If this does happen, the cost to them could be several hundred pounds in abortive legal and survey fees and two to three weeks wasted time.

A survey report is not transferable and a buyer would have no legal comeback on the surveyor if the report was later found to be inaccurate. However, the availability of a survey report can do a great deal to allay a buyer's fears and it could prove to be well worth its cost. A survey report is particularly valuable if you are selling a house that is large, old or in poor condition.

# 5

# ARRANGING THE VALUATION APPOINTMENT

When you telephone to arrange a valuation appointment, the agent will want to ask you a number of questions. Beware. It is probably not in your best interest to answer them all at this time. The likely questions can be divided into three categories.

### Questions about the property

The agent will ask for a detailed description of your property. He needs this information in order to research its value prior to his visit. You should describe your property accurately and thoroughly, paying particular attention to any unusual features such as an extension.

### Questions about you

The agent will also ask for a lot of background information about you. He will want to know the reason for your move, your anticipated time-scale and whether you have already contacted other agents. The agent's purpose in asking such questions is to ascertain whether you are serious about moving or whether you just want a valuation. Your answers to these questions will determine how seriously your enquiry is taken and also, very often, the seniority of the member of staff sent out to see you. For this reason these questions must be answered with some care. In particular

- Never admit to being in a hurry to sell. This could mean a lower valuation.

- Always say that you will be inviting several agents around before deciding who to instruct on a sole agency basis (a more senior member of staff will often be sent to sell the firm's service against competition).

## Questions about the property's value

Some agents will ask you what price you are hoping to achieve for your property over the telephone. If you reveal this at this stage there is a real danger that the agent will tell you the price that you want to hear instead of giving you a properly researched valuation. You should therefore decline to answer this question at this time. Say something like 'I do have a price in mind but I should like to hear your opinion first.'

Having answered the agent's questions, the next thing to do is to agree on a time for the appointment. Your valuation appointment is an extremely important occasion, and it is my belief that it is an occasion where two heads are better than one. If you have a partner, then both of you should be present. If not you might consider asking a trusted friend to sit through each appointment with you.

The amount of time each agent will wish to spend with you will vary widely but, to be on the safe side 1½ hours should be allowed between appointments. It is embarrassing for everyone if the next agent arrives before the previous one has left. The best time for an appointment is undoubtedly a weekday when most agents will have more time to explain their service fully. On no account should an agent be invited to undertake a valuation after dark. Artificial light makes a property look so different that accurate valuation is impossible.

Finally, do not be frightened to stand firm on your preferred appointment times. Agents often try to sound busier than they are in order to impress potential clients and may be able to move 'another appointment' if you insist on a particular time.

# 6

# THE VALUATION APPOINTMENT

## BACKGROUND AND FIRST IMPRESSIONS

Estate agency is a profession that is full of eccentrics. It is therefore important to resist the temptation to judge each agent on the basis of first impressions alone. The dishevelled-looking chap who arrives by bicycle, ten minutes late for the appointment, could very easily be the best agent for the job.

After exchanging pleasantries, the agent will probably wish to start the appointment by sitting down with you to discuss the background to your move. During this part of the appointment the agent will be trying to establish three things:

- How serious are you about moving?

- What is your time-scale?

- Why are you moving?

The experienced estate agent will make this stage of the appointment seem like nothing more than an informal exchange of pleasantries but in fact every single question will have a purpose. For example the purpose of a question like 'are you moving with work?' might be to find out if your company will be paying the fees so that a higher than usual commission rate may be quoted. Your answers to all such questions should reassure the agent that you are serious about moving. However, you must at the same time be very careful not to say anything that may later prejudice your negotiating position. If, for example, you are desperate to sell your property quickly, you should keep this to yourself, at very least until an asking price and a commission level have been agreed and preferably until the property has been on the market for a couple of weeks. If you do not, you may find that you are quoted a lower asking price, an increased commission level, or both!

Having established the background to your move, the agent will next wish to look round the property. I would recommend that he should be allowed to do so alone. During this initial inspection tour the agent will value your property by comparing it with all the others that he has seen. This process requires great concentration and the valuation will probably be more accurate if the agent is not obliged to make small talk during his inspection.

On his return the agent should be ready to discuss his valuation with you. I say should because just occasionally you will come across an agent who is unwilling to discuss his valuation without first discussing it with his colleagues back at the office. If the property is very large or unusual then there is some justification for this. If it is not you should ask the agent bluntly why he feels unable to give you a valuation on the spot. The most likely reasons are inexperience or lack of preparation. If you suspect that either is the case you should find another agent.

## AGREEING AN ASKING PRICE

### Beware of the agent who overvalues

The worst possible way to choose an estate agent is to instruct the one that quotes the highest asking price. Unfortunately this is exactly how many home owners make their decision. A minority of estate agents exploit this by deliberately over-valuing the properties that they see in order to get instructions. Once instructed, they will try to persuade the client to reduce the asking price in the hope that the property can still be sold before the end of the sole agency period. Such agents should be avoided like the plague. Fortunately they are very easy to spot.

An agent who deliberately overvalues will spend the whole valuation appointment trying to find out the price that you want to hear. The least subtle will ask you directly for the price that you are hoping to achieve. Most will try to find out by more subtle methods.

One common method is to ask you how long you have owned the house and how much you originally paid for it. By applying the appropriate annual adjustment factors the agent will be able to calculate the likely present value. An alternative method is to ask how much you are intending to spend on your next house and then later on by how much you are planning to increase your present mortgage. Some very simple mathematics will give the agent the price that you are hoping to achieve for your present house. A more subtle technique involves the agent mentioning the prices of a number of other houses that have been sold recently. Each time a price is mentioned the agent will watch closely for your reaction. Each time you look disappointed, he will raise his 'valuation' for your property until he is sure that you will be happy with the figure that he gives you.

You have absolutely nothing to gain from revealing your assessment of the property's value before you have heard the agent's opinion and my advice would be to respond to all such questions by saying something like 'I really would like to hear your valuation before I discuss my expectations with you.' Faced with this response the agent will have no choice but to give his own opinion of value.

## Control your reaction

However disappointed you are by the agent's figure, it is important not to show it at this stage. In order to obtain the maximum benefit from the agent's experience, you must first work calmly through four further stages:

### Stage 1 Confirmation

Some agents try to leave themselves room for manoeuvre by saying that the property is worth between £50–£55,000. It is important to try to pin the agent down to a precise figure. Try asking him in what circumstances he would expect to achieve both the lower and the higher figure.

### Stage 2 Qualification

The main purpose of this stage is to prevent an agent from trying to wriggle out of his original valuation when challenged. He may try to do this using words such as:

■   My original figure of £65,000 is the price I expect to obtain after negotiation. The asking price of course would be much higher.

To avoid this you should ask the agent to confirm every aspect of his valuation by asking questions such as:

■   What would be your recommended asking price?

■   What price would you expect to obtain after negotiation?

■   How long would you expect it to take to find a buyer at this price?

### Stage 3 Justification

Ask the agent to explain to you the exact process by which he arrived at his valuation. In particular ask him which comparable properties he took into account before arriving at his final figure. A good agent should be able to justify his valuation without hesitation, by referring to at least three comparable properties. A really good agent will have brought the sales particulars of all comparable properties with him to the appointment.

### Stage 4 Negotiation

Once you have heard both the agent's valuation and his justification for it, you can safely reveal your own expectation and the process by which you arrived at it. The process of negotiation which is likely to follow is probably best demonstrated by the use of some fictitious case studies.

### Case Study A: UNDERVALUATION – VENDOR CONCEDES

Agent's initial valuation £90,000: recommended asking price £93,950.

Vendor    I'm sorry to tell you that your valuation is £5,000 less than I was hoping to achieve and I'd like to tell you how I arrived at my figure. I have two justifications:

(1)    The property opposite which is identical to mine was sold eight weeks ago for £96,000.

(2)    I believe that number 86, which has no garage, was also sold last month for £89,000.

On this evidence I really do expect to get £95,000 for mine.

Agent    The original price agreed for the house opposite was indeed £96,000 but the building society valuer downvalued it on survey to £90,000 and that is what it sold for. I therefore stand by my valuation of £90,000.

Vendor    But number 89 sold for £89,950 and it doesn't have a garage.

Agent    When number 89 was sold the house opposite was for sale at £99,950. This made 86 seem good value. Now that it is known that the house opposite sold for £90,000 this sets a ceiling on the price achievable in the road.

Vendor    I accept your argument but I would like to quote an initial asking price of £96,950 not £93,950.

Agent     I believe that the price would discourage potential viewers.

Vendor    All right, then £95,950.

Agent     I will try it at that figure for 14 days but we must review the price after that.

## CASE STUDY B: UNDERVALUATION – AGENT CONCEDES

Agent's initial valuation £65,000; recommended asking price £66,950.

Vendor    I am disappointed by your figure. Number 12 sold at £69,000 and number 19 is for sale at £69,950.

Agent     We sold a house in the next road a few weeks ago for £65,000. I believe my valuation is correct.

Vendor    You didn't refer to number 12 or to number 19 when citing your comparable evidence. I have to ask whether you took them into account in your valuation.

Agent     We didn't handle those sales.

Vendor    That doesn't answer my question.

Agent     I have based my valuation on the house which we sold in the next road.

Vendor    In view of the price achieved for number 12, I should like to quote £69,950 for my property. Would you be prepared to take it on at that figure?

Agent     Yes.

Vendor    Very well. If I instruct you it will be at £69,950.

## CASE STUDY C: OVERVALUATION – AGENT CONCEDES

Agent's initial valuation £45,000; recommended asking price £46,750.

**Vendor**  My own valuation was £3,000 less than yours. I based it on two other identical flats in the block, numbers 4 and 22, both of which have sold for £42,000 within the last three months. Could you explain to me again how you arrived at your figure.

**Agent**  The even numbered flats are at the front of the block. They always seem to sell for less.

**Vendor**  That wasn't true when I bought this flat. What has changed since?

**Agent**  I don't know, but it is generally true.

**Vendor**  When did you last sell a flat in this block?

**Agent**  I've been in the agency for five years. The company must have sold loads.

**Vendor**  How about you personally?

**Agent**  Well – I only moved to this branch a couple of months ago.

**Vendor**  Whilst I would like to get £45,000 I don't believe that I can do it in the time available. If I instruct you it will be at a lower figure, but thank you for your advice.

### The final decision
Always remember that the final decision on an asking price is yours and yours alone. There is absolutely nothing to stop you instructing an agent at an asking price that is different from the one recommended. The agent's job is to advise, your job is to weigh up advice from as many different sources as possible and to decide. No one else should make that decision for you.

## ASSESSING THE AGENT'S SALES PRESENTATION
Giving an accurate valuation is one thing, achieving that price is quite another. Your decision as to which agent to instruct cannot therefore be made on the basis of the valuation alone.

Once an asking price has been agreed, the estate agent should, of his own accord, tell you more about the service that his company offers. It is best to leave the agent to highlight the key features of his service but if necessary you should prompt him in order to ensure that the following areas are covered:

### 1. Experience

- How long has he personally been in the business?
- How long has he worked in the local area?
- How long has he worked for his present employer?
- How experienced are the other members of his team?

### 2. Company Background

- Who owns the business?
- How long has the firm been established?

### 3. Advertising

- Where does the firm advertise?
- Do the advertisements have any special features (e.g. colour photographs)?

### 4. Property Particulars

- Does the company use colour photographs on its particulars?

### 5. Coverage

- Does the company have offices in other local towns?
- If so, will your property details be available there.

### 6. Opening hours

- What are the usual opening hours?
- Is the office staffed by full-time people at weekends?

### 7. Sales Methods

- Are buyers usually contacted by telephone or by post?
- Will the agent accompany viewings or will you be left to show buyers round yourself?

### 8. Qualification/Security

- How does the agency check to ensure that buyers are genuine?
- How will they check that buyers can afford to buy your property before arranging an appointment?

## 9. Sales Progressing

- What action will the agent take to ensure that your sale reaches a satisfactory conclusion?

## 10. Recent Results

- Has the agent recently sold other properties in your area?
- How many houses do they usually sell each month? (They might not tell you but there is no harm in asking.)

## 11. Testimonials

- Can the agent show you testimonials from satisfied clients?

By the end of this part of the interview you will probably have a very good idea about whether you wish to instruct the agent or not. The final factor in you decision will be the commission level.

# 7

# NEGOTIATING THE FEE

The maxim 'you get what you pay for' is true for most things in life and estate agency is no exception. If you are quoted an unexpectedly low fee the first thing to do is to check that you are being quoted for a full estate agency service. You will very often find that the lower fee is in fact being quoted by a property shop or by an agent who operates on an exclusive agency basis. (See Chapter 9.)

## PROPERTY SHOPS VERSUS CONVENTIONAL ESTATE AGENTS

Property shops charge much lower fees than estate agents. They are able to do this because they charge their fee at the point of instruction and keep it regardless of whether a sale is achieved or not. The inherent disadvantage of paying an up front fee is that the property shop has no financial incentive to sell your house. It is probably because of this that the success rate of most property shops is lower than that of most estate agents. Taking everything into account a conventional estate agent is usually likely to offer better value for money.

## RESPONDING TO A LOWER THAN EXPECTED FEE

If you are quoted a low fee by a conventional estate agent, you must establish how he is able to undercut his competitors. You might say something like 'The fee that you have quoted is half a percent less than your main competitors. Could I ask how you are able to offer the same service at a lower price?'

On closer examination you will often find that the lower fee is financed by less advertising, fewer staff, cheaper premises or some other such economy. If this is the case you should weigh up very carefully how these economies might affect the agent's ability to achieve the best price for your property.

## RESPONDING TO A HIGHER THAN EXPECTED FEE

If you are quoted a fee that is higher than expected, you should challenge it firmly but politely. You might say something like 'I am impressed by your service but your fee is half a percent more than I've been quoted elsewhere. How can you justify this differential?' Faced with such a challenge the effective agent might try one of two approaches:

(a)  He might try to justify the differential by pointing out further features of his service which are not offered by his competitors e.g. colour advertising or longer opening hours.

(b)  He might argue that the same negotiation techniques which enable him to obtain premium fee levels from his clients will also enable him to achieve a premium price for your property!

Both arguments have some merit. It is for you to decide whether you believe that superior marketing or superior negotiation techniques will indeed lead to a higher sale price but my experience is that they often do.

The less effective agent will respond to his fee level being challenged in one of two other ways:

(a)  He will immediately match the lower fee. If he does this you must ask whether he would give in so easily when negotiating an offer for your property with a potential purchaser.

(b)  He will suggest that the extra commission is added on to your asking price. This is quite indefensible. If the property is really worth more why did the agent not say so sooner? If it is not then you will end up paying his whole fee anyway.

## SOME NON-CONVENTIONAL FEE ARRANGEMENTS

Most agents express their fee as a percentage of the selling price but there is no need for the fee to be calculated in this way. The following alternatives may be appropriate in different circumstances. Their introduction may also often help to resolve fee negotiations that have become deadlocked:

### The split percentage fee

Most of an agent's skill is used to persuade a purchaser to increase his offer by the last few thousand pounds. This arrangement recognises this by giving an agent a much higher reward if he achieves a premium price. A split fee arrangement works like this:

**Conventional fee**

| | |
|---|---|
| Asking price | £109,950 |
| Expected sales price | £100,000 |
| Fee Payable 100,000 x 2% | £   2,000 |

**Split fee**

| | |
|---|---|
| Asking price | £109,950 |
| Fee agreement | 1½% of the first £95,000 and 10% of any balance achieved above this figure |
| Price achieved | £105,000 |
| Fee payable | £ 95,000 x 1½% =      £1,425 |
| + | £ 10,000 x 10% =      £1,000 |
| Total fee payable | £2,425 |

In this example the agent is £425 better off, but the vendor is £4,265 better off!

This sort of arrangement gives the agent a tremendous incentive to achieve a premium price and can be an excellent arrangement for both parties.

**The fixed fee**

It is agreed that a fee of £X will be paid regardless of what price is achieved for the property. This arrangement would most commonly be used for very expensive properties, or at the agent's instigation, for a very cheap property (e.g. a mobile home) where he wishes to charge a minimum fee but is embarrassed to quote this as 10% of the selling price. Fixed fees have their place but the drawback is that the agent has no financial incentive to achieve a higher price for the vendor.

**The part up front fee**

An agent knows that he will only sell approximately 50% of all the houses that he takes on. The remainder will be withdrawn by vendors who decide not to sell after all or will be sold by another agent. The cost of marketing properties that are not sold is considerable and ultimately this cost has to be recovered from clients who do sell. For this reason agents are often prepared to make a substantial reduction in their commission in return for a relatively small non-refundable advance payment.

For example:

> Usual fee 2% selling price of £100,000 Fee = £2,000
> Alternative £500 advance payment
> 1% fee payable on sale
> Total fee payable £1,500
> Saving to client £500.

This method is only to be recommended if you are absolutely sure that you want to sell your property and if you are also certain about your choice of agent.

## The personal bonus

By arrangement with the office manager, you may be able to agree to pay a personal bonus to the individual negotiator who sells your property. This arrangement is particularly appropriate if you need to sell your property quickly. Increasing the agent's commission from 2 to 2½% would have little effect on the way that the agent marketed your property. Offering a ½% bonus to the individual negotiator who sells the property could do a great deal to ensure that your property is given priority.

I would stress that such arrangements should only be made with the full knowledge and approval of the manager and/or the proprietor. You must also make it clear to the negotiator who receives the bonus that he or she will be responsible for paying income tax on the monies paid.

After considering every possible alternative fee structure and engaging in five or ten minutes of lively negotiation you will be almost ready to make your final choice of agent.

# 8

# THE FINAL DECISION

At the end of the valuation appointment, the agent will probably ask you to make a decision on the spot. You should not do so for several reasons. Firstly, however good the first agent is, the next one might be even better. Having taken the trouble to compile a short list, you really should see everyone on it. Secondly, by delaying your decision for a couple of days you will get one last opportunity to test each agent's qualities of persistence and determination by seeing how vigorously they follow the appointment up. Thirdly, a number of important decisions have yet to be made about the terms and duration of the agency agreement. Such decisions are best not made under pressure.

At the end of the appointment thank the agent for his advice and say politely but firmly that you will be making a final decision within a few days. Most agents will accept this without further argument. The really effective agent, however, will not take no for an answer so easily and may try several more times to get a decision from you on the spot. This is an occasion when determination and persistence should be admired. The agent who tries hard to win your instructions is likely to be equally persistent when persuading potential purchasers to view your house.

The really skilled agent will seem to have an answer for every objection that you raise, for example:

Customer:     I'd like to think it over.

Agent:        Of course, but exactly what do you need to think about before deciding?

Customer:     I've got one more agent to see.

Agent:            Of course, but exactly what are you hoping they will offer which I don't?

It can be surprisingly difficult to resist a determined onslaught from a really good sales person but resist you must. You cannot be sure of making the right decision under such pressure. The best way to counter such sales techniques is to keep repeating calmly but firmly that you will not make such an important decision on the spot.

Once the final agent has left, you are at last in a position to make your final decision. Often one agent will come out head and shoulders above the others. If this is not the case, it may be helpful to compare the best two or three agents using the comparison table at the end of this section.

# 9

# AGENCY TERMS

## COMMON AGENCY TERMS

### Southern England

There are four types of agency agreement in use in Southern England:

**Sole Agency** means that just one agent is instructed to market a property. It is common these days for agents to ask for a minimum period of sole agency – an initial period of eight to twelve weeks would be typical. If you choose to instruct an agent on a sole agency basis, you will probably be asked to sign a sole agency agreement. You should be aware that this is a legally binding contract which will prevent you from instructing any other agent during the sole agency period. If you break the agreement you may be liable to pay two lots of estate agents' commission, one to the original sole agent and one to the selling agent.

**Joint Sole Agency** means that two agents agree to share the agency commission regardless of which one of them achieves a sale. The most common circumstance for a joint sole agency agreement is where an expensive or unusual property needs to be marketed by a London agent in addition to a local one. Fee levels for Joint Sole Agency are significantly higher than for a conventional sole agency.

**Multiple Agency** means that one or more agents are instructed to sell a property on the basis that whichever achieves a sale keeps the entire fee. Multiple agency is a very combative and inefficient way of doing business and because of this some agents will not accept instructions at all on this basis.

**Sole Selling Rights** work on a similar basis to Sole Agency. The difference is that the agent is entitled to receive a fee if the property is sold within the agency period *even if the agent was not responsible for achieving the sale*. If you sold your house to your brother, a fee would still technically be payable. There is no justification for any agent to ask for sole selling rights and you should not agree to instruct anyone on this basis. Thankfully the use of sole selling rights agreements is now extremely rare.

### Northern England

The agency system in Northern England (defined as approximately north of Birmingham) operates in a different way. The four types of agency agreement detailed above are all available, but in Northern England Multiple Agency Agreements are much rarer. A second difference is that two types of sole agency agreement are in use.

**Inclusive Agency** This is the standard southern sole agency system where a fee is payable only if the property is sold.

**Exclusive Agency** This means that you will be liable to pay the agent's out-of-pocket expenses in addition to sales commission. These expenses will include items such as advertising, photography and the cost of erecting a For Sale board. You will be liable to pay the agent's expenses *whether or not the property is sold*. You may also be liable to pay a withdrawal fee if the property is withdrawn from the market for any reason.

## CHOOSING THE MOST APPROPRIATE TYPE OF AGENCY AGREEMENT

### Southern England

### Circumstances where a Sole Agency is appropriate

Sole agency has four important advantages over a multiple agency agreement.

- **It is cheaper** Because a sole agent has a greater chance of receiving a fee he can afford to charge a lower rate of commission. Sole agency fees are typically 20 – 50% lower than multiple agency rates.

- **You will usually get a better service** Agents who are instructed on a multiple agency basis are often reluctant to spend money advertising and marketing a property which might be sold by a competitor. Your property will probably get far more exposure if you instruct an agent on a sole agency basis.

- **No risk of overexposure** If a potential purchaser is offered the same property by ten different agents, he may wonder what is wrong with it.

There is no doubt that overexposure can be counter-productive. A sole agency will avoid this problem.

- **No conflict of interest** Imagine a situation where an agent receives a low offer for your property. If he is acting as your sole agent he can safely advise you to refuse it. If he is acting on a multiple agency basis he might be tempted to try to persuade you to accept the low offer to ensure that he gets the fee, not his competitor.

For these reasons I would advise most sellers to start off by instructing an agent on a sole agency basis. The exceptions are detailed below.

### Circumstances where a Joint Sole Agency is appropriate

People who are looking for a very expensive or unusual house are usually prepared to consider properties in a much larger geographical area than most ordinary purchasers.

A purchaser who wishes to buy a country estate, a listed property or perhaps a riverside property, might be prepared to look at anything within, say, two hours travelling time of London. Such purchasers could not possibly register with all the agents in such a large area and most will therefore register their requirements only with agents in London and the major provincial cities. Unless your property is being offered for sale at these locations it will be overlooked.

If your property is truly unusual, it is well worth the extra expense of a joint sole agency. If it is not, the extra commission payable (typically 30 – 50% more) is unlikely to be recovered.

### Circumstances where a Multiple Agency is appropriate

Despite the inherent disadvantages of multiple agency there are some circumstances in which it might be appropriate:

- **For village or suburban properties** Some village and suburban properties require exposure in more than one local town or centre. If you are selling a property in a village that is equidistant from three or more larger towns, you might consider instructing one agent in each centre on a multiple agency basis. Where there are only two local towns a joint sole agency agreement may be more appropriate.

- **When no agent in the town is outstanding** Perhaps you can't make up your mind between instructing a small enthusiastic independent agent or a larger but apparently less efficient one. If you really can't decide, a multiple agency might be appropriate.

- **When a property has already been unsuccessfully marketed by a sole agent** This is the most common reason for instructing an agent on a multiple agency basis. Although multiple agency is often appropriate in these circumstances, you should also consider sacking the first agent and entering into a second sole agency agreement with another firm.

The one thing to avoid at all costs is the temptation to instruct every agent in the town. In a town with twenty agents there is nothing to be gained from instructing more than two or three. If you instruct all twenty, your property will be over-exposed and your chances of selling it seriously reduced.

## Northern England

### Circumstances where an Exclusive Sole Agency is appropriate

As an exclusive agency client you will be responsible for paying all out-of-pocket expenses involved with marketing your property whether it is sold or not. As an inclusive agency client you will, through higher fee levels, end up paying not only the costs of marketing your property, but also a proportion of the cost of marketing other properties that were withdrawn from the market leaving the agent with unrecoverable costs to bear. For this reason exclusive agency is usually the most cost-effective choice for the committed vendor.

### Circumstances where an Inclusive Sole Agency is appropriate

There are two circumstances where an inclusive agency might be appropriate:

(1)  When you are not certain about an agent's ability.

(2)  Where there is a chance that you might change your mind about moving. (In which case is it really fair to waste the agent's time and money?)

# 10

# INSTRUCTING AN ESTATE AGENT

## GIVING DETAILED INSTRUCTIONS

Having made your decision regarding which agent to instruct and on what terms, you should next clarify in your mind your detailed instructions to that agent. In particular you need to make a decision on:

### Initial asking price

Bearing in mind all the evidence that you have seen and heard, are you certain about you initial asking price? If it is too high, it will spoil the momentum of the marketing campaign and may demotivate the agent. On the other hand, if it is too low, it will be all but impossible to raise it later.

### Period of sole agency

What period of sole agency are you prepared to give? If it is too short (say less than six weeks) the agent may be reluctant to spend money marketing a property that he might not sell. If it is too long (say more than twelve weeks) you run the risk of being tied to an ineffective agent.

### Subagencies

Some agents will invite other agents in the town to act on a subagency basis. This means that they will also offer your property for sale and if they sell it will receive half the commission. My opinion is that subagencies are usually not in the best interests of the seller, mainly because of the risk of overexposure. If you are prepared to allow your agent to instruct subagents, you should insist that the number is strictly limited and ask for a list of all subagents before they are instructed.

## For Sale board

Approximately 25% of all applicants are attracted by For Sale boards and a board will therefore undoubtedly increase your chances of selling. If you are reluctant to have one, you should examine your objections most carefully. Is the risk of the odd unwanted caller a price worth paying for a quicker sale?

## Keys

If at all possible you should give your agent a key. This is even more important if you are out at work in the daytime. A surprising number of people wish to view during working hours and many will not bother to try to make another appointment if they cannot view immediately.

Having made a decision on all the above issues you are now ready to telephone the lucky agent to inform him of your decision and arrange a final appointment to put the house on the market.

## INFORMING THE UNSUCCESSFUL AGENTS

It is well worth spending five or ten minutes telephoning or writing to the unsuccessful agents to inform them of your decision. You might need their services in the future and a short courtesy call at this time will make it far easier to go back to them in the future should the need arise.

## THE SOLE AGENCY AGREEMENT

The agency agreement is a legal contract and you should read it most carefully before signing. You should not hesitate to ask the agent to explain any clause that is unclear. If you are not happy with any aspect of the agreement you should refuse to sign it on the spot and take it to your solicitor or to a trusted friend for clarification.

A typical agency agreement will include the following:

- **Confirmation of fee level** Check that this is what has been agreed. Also check any multiple agency rate. It will be far easier to negotiate a multiple agency rate now, when the sole agency period is being agreed, than later when it is being ended.

- **Confirmation of asking price** Double check the figure agreed.

- **Confirmation of agency terms** Check that you are signing for a sole or multiple agency as appropriate.

■ **Sole agency period** Check that this is as agreed. Check also whether a notice period is hidden in the small print.

■ **Authority to pay fees** Many agency agreements contain a clause that gives your solicitor authority to pay the agent's fees from the sale proceeds.

■ **Offer of 'connected services'** Estate agents must by law inform you of any service that might be offered to potential purchasers such as mortgage advice, removals or the sale of their own property.

■ **For Sale board** Many agency agreements include a clause authorising the erection of a For Sale board. Delete this clause if you don't want one.

■ **Race Relations Act** Many agreements include a clause that confirms that you will not discriminate against potential purchasers on account of their colour or race.

■ **Subagencies** Many agreements include a clause that gives the agent authority to instruct subagents. Delete this if appropriate.

■ **Property Misdescriptions Act** You may be asked to sign a separate form relating to the Property Misdescriptions Act.

■ **Other specific instructions** You should insist that any additional instructions given to the agent are recorded in writing on the sole agency agreement to prevent misunderstandings.

A sample sole agency agreement is shown in Appendix 1.

## SUMMARY

All estate agents are not the same.

This comparison table will help you to assess the agents that you have seen. Give each agent a score out of ten in each category.

| INITIAL IMPRESSIONS | | Agent | | | | |
|---|---|---|---|---|---|---|
| MARKETING CAMPAIGN | | 1 | 2 | 3 | 4 | 5 |
| Newspaper advertising | | | | | | |
| 1 | Size of advert | | | | | |
| 2 | Quality of publication | | | | | |
| 3 | Position | | | | | |
| 4 | Frequency | | | | | |
| 5 | Layout | | | | | |
| 6 | Colour/black & white | | | | | |
| 7 | Variety/content | | | | | |
| 8 | Sale board presence | | | | | |
| 9 | Office position | | | | | |
| 10 | Overall impression | | | | | |
| CUSTOMER SERVICE | | | | | | |
| 11 | Initial response | | | | | |
| 12 | Rapport | | | | | |
| 13 | Qualification | | | | | |
| 14 | Sales ability | | | | | |
| | Quality of property details | | | | | |
| 15 | Promptness | | | | | |
| 16 | Presentation | | | | | |
| 17 | Telephone follow-up | | | | | |
| 18 | Ongoing follow-up | | | | | |
| 19 | Persistence | | | | | |
| Overall impression | | | | | | |

Continued....

| MARKETING CAMPAIGN | 1 | 2 | 3 | 4 | 5 |
|---|---|---|---|---|---|
| THE VALUATION APPOINTMENT | | | | | |
| 1 First impressions | | | | | |
| 2 Thoroughness of background research | | | | | |
| 3 Accuracy of valuation | | | | | |
| 4 Presentation of valuation | | | | | |
| 5 Sales presentation | | | | | |
| 6 Experience | | | | | |
| 7 Company background | | | | | |
| 8 Advertising | | | | | |
| 9 Quality of particulars | | | | | |
| 10 Coverage | | | | | |
| 11 Opening hours | | | | | |
| 12 Sales methods | | | | | |
| 13 Buyer qualification | | | | | |
| 14 Sales progressing | | | | | |
| 15 Recent results | | | | | |
| 16 Testimonials | | | | | |
| Fee Levels % | | | | | |
| Non-conventional fee alternatives | | | | | |
| Minimum period of sole agency requested (weeks) | | | | | |
| Overall score | | | | | |

# SECTION 2

# FINDING A BUYER

# 11

# PREPARING THE PARTICULARS

The first thing that your estate agent will do after instructions have been confirmed is to prepare the property particulars.

The particulars will play an extremely important role in persuading potential purchasers to view your property. It is, therefore, worth going to some considerable trouble to ensure that they show the property to its best advantage.

The following tips will help to ensure that your particulars stand out from the crowd.

## GENERAL LAYOUT

The typical purchaser will receive several dozen sets of particulars during his property search. Because of this, your particulars will need to make their impact within just a few seconds. Sloppy photocopying or poor layout will reduce significantly the number of potential buyers that decide to view and should not be tolerated.

## THE PHOTOGRAPH

Ninety percent of purchasers will look at the photograph before they look at anything else. If they don't like what they see, they will reject your property out of hand. It is therefore vital to ensure that the photograph shows your property in the very best possible light.

### Choosing an angle

The angle that the photograph is taken from should be chosen with particular care. Most photographs show the front elevation. However, if your property looks better from another angle, there is no reason why the photograph should not show the back or the side.

### Colour *v.* black and white

The photograph itself really should be in colour. If your estate agent does not use colour photographs on his details, it is worth considering paying the extra cost of colour photography yourself.

### Size

The size of the photograph is important. A photograph that measures 5" x 7" or larger will make a far greater impact than the traditional mini print.

### Recentness

The last point to make about the photograph is that it must be recent. A photograph of a property covered in snow, sent out in August will convey the message 'and they *still* haven't sold it!'

### Internal photographs

Internal photographs can play a useful role in persuading people to view a property. If your property has any particularly attractive internal features, you should ask your estate agent to include an internal photograph on the details.

### Photographing ugly properties

Some houses are not particularly photogenic. Some houses are just plain ugly. If your property falls into this category (be honest with yourself here) it may be better to include only internal photographs on the property particulars.

## THE TEXT

You must always remember that the purpose of the property particulars is to persuade people to view your property, not to sell the property itself. You should therefore be ruthless about removing from the text all unnecessary information. In particular you should take care to remove any trivial details that might discourage people from viewing. For example, reference to a pink bathroom suite would do nothing to increase a property's saleablity but could, very easily, put some purchasers off.

## PROPERTY PARTICULARS AND THE LAW

Estate agents used to be famous for their ability to make even the most undesirable property sound like a palace. All such hyperbole was ended by the passing of the Property Misdescriptions Act in April 1993.

The Property Misdescriptions Act made it a *criminal* offence for an estate agent (but not a homeowner) to misdescribe a property that is offered for sale. The penalties for non-compliance are severe and even a minor transgression can lead to a substantial fine and a criminal record for the estate agent.

The passing of the Property Misdescriptions Act has led to far-reaching changes in estate agency practice and this has affected vendors in two ways. The first effect of the act is that estate agents' details have become far shorter and less colourful than they used to be. Estate agents dare not make any statement that cannot be verified. Thus a phrase such as 'the house is ten minutes walk from the shops' has either been changed to 'the property is 637 metres from the nearest shop' or, more commonly, omitted altogether.

The second effect of the act has been to cause considerable delays in putting properties onto the market. The reason for this is that estate agents now have a statutory obligation to verify all claims that they wish to make about a property. For example, if a property has been rewired the agent will need to see a detailed invoice for the work. If a property has damp guarantees the agent will need to see a copy of the guarantee. If a property has a 67-year lease, the agent will need to see a copy of the lease to verify this. Many homeowners do not have such documents readily available and the delays that occur whilst the documents are obtained can cause considerable inconvenience and frustration. If you find yourself in this situation, you will need to make a choice between waiting for the documents to be obtained, and marketing your property with all reference to the unsubstantiated facts omitted from the details.

# 12

# OBTAINING VIEWINGS

## WHAT SHOULD THE AGENT BE DOING?

Once the house is on the market your agent should start earning his fee by persuading as many people as possible to view it. He will try to achieve this in a number of ways.

### By telephone

The agent should have a number of 'Hot Applicants' on his register. These are people who are prepared to view without seeing the details and are in a position to proceed with a purchase immediately. (First time buyers or own property sold.) The agent should telephone these people to obtain viewings *before* the details are sent out. These are the hottest applicants of all. One of them may wish to buy your property immediately.

### By post

During the preceding two to three months the agent's general marketing campaign should have attracted a number of applicants. Within the first few days, the agent should send a set of particulars to every applicant that he has in the price range. Sending details alone is not enough. The effective agent will also telephone each of these applicants a few days after they receive the details to obtain feedback and to attempt to persuade them to view.

### Circulating details to other branches

If you have instructed a multi-office agent, details of your property should be circulated to all the neighbouring branches. This will not always happen automatically. Inter-branch rivalry often means that neighbouring branches end up competing with each other rather than cooperating. You must ensure that such inter-branch rivalries do not affect your chances of obtaining a sale. You can check this by doing two things. Firstly, ask what commission sharing arrangements are in place in the event of your property being sold by another branch (do they seem fair to you?). Secondly, try phoning the neighbouring branches posing as an applicant looking for a property in the same price range as yours and see whether your property is mentioned.

### Erection of a For Sale board

A For Sale board is an important marketing tool. Something like a quarter of all sales are achieved due to a board. If you really want to sell your house for the best possible price in the shortest possible time, then you need a For Sale board. The board may encourage the odd unwanted visitor to knock on the door without an appointment, but such people can easily be turned away and this small intrusion is a price well worth paying for the extra interest that a board will generate.

### How long should it take to find a buyer?

It is, of course, impossible to predict how long it will take to find a buyer. The report produced by Black Horse Agencies, that appears in Appendix 2 gives some idea of the average time that it takes to sell a property. However, there is a big difference between the average time it takes to sell a property and how long it takes the average property to sell. The reason for this is that a property that takes two years to sell will have a disproportionate effect on the average.

Statistically the time when a property in Southern England is most likely to sell is during the first four weeks of going onto the market. During this period the agent is able to work on all the potential buyers who have registered during the preceding few months. By the end of the first month you should certainly have had a number of viewings and you may well have achieved a sale. If you have not, you should begin to consider the possibility that your property is going to prove more difficult to sell than you thought.

In Northern England, as the report shows, the market tends to operate more slowly. If you are selling a property in the North you should allow eight to twelve weeks for the initial marketing campaign to run its course.

If you have not achieved a sale within these time-scales, you should begin to consider the possibility that your property is going to prove more difficult to sell than you first thought.

# 13

# THE ADVERTISING CAMPAIGN

The advertising campaign is a very important part of the overall marketing plan. The following hints will help to ensure that you get maximum benefit from the advertisements that are run for your property.

## Page position

Certain positions on the page attract far more interest than others. In general terms the rules are:

- Right-hand pages are better than left-hand pages.

- The top of the page is better than the bottom of the page.

- The boxes at the edge of a page get more interest than those in the centre of the page.

This can be shown as a diagram:

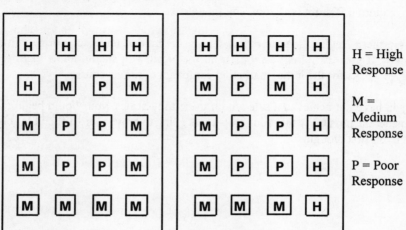

H = High Response

M = Medium Response

P = Poor Response

Try to insist on a good position when your property is advertised. A good position could double or treble the response.

## The photograph

Potential buyers will look at the photograph and decide whether or not they want to view the property within seconds. It is therefore essential to choose a photograph that shows the property in its best light. If you have any reservations about the photograph you should not hesitate to ask your agent to take another one.

## Subsequent photographs

Many buyers have a memory like an elephant for houses that have been previously advertised. If they recognise a photograph that they have seen before, they will move straight on to the next property without even pausing to read the text.

The golden rule therefore is never to use the same photograph twice. Subsequent advertisements should use a photograph taken from a different angle, an internal shot or perhaps a rear view of the property.

## Advertising an ugly property

There is little point in photographing an ugly property. If your house looks like a concrete prison block you should consider:

- Advertising it with an internal photograph.

- Advertising it without a photograph at all.

- Asking your agent to advertise a prettier property in the same price range as your own on the understanding that all respondents will be told about your property as well as the one advertised.

## The text

The purpose of an advertisement is to generate enquiries. If everything that a potential purchaser needs to know about the property is included in the advertisement then they will have no reason to contact the agent. The effective agent will counter this by withholding a vital piece of information about each property. This might be the location, the price or the number of bedrooms.

By advertising in this way, the agent can increase quite significantly the number of enquiries that each advertisement generates. Once a prospective purchaser is on the phone the agent will have a much better chance of persuading him to view the property.

## Text of subsequent advertisements

An advertisement that has been run once is stale. If the same advertisement is run again it will achieve a much reduced response. You should, therefore, never use the same text twice. Subsequent advertisements should be rewritten from scratch and should highlight different features of the property. For example:

| | |
|---|---|
| **First advertisement**<br>Appeals to family with children | **Close to Queens School**<br>This three bedroom semi-detached property is situated in a quiet cul-de-sac and is very convenient to Queens School.<br><br>It has three bedrooms and a 60' south facing garden.<br><br>Price £69,950. |
| **Second advertisement**<br>Appeals to professional couple | **First class commuter access**<br>This three bedroom semi-detached property is within two minutes of the M1, Junction 10 and less than half a mile from the mainline station.<br><br>The accommodation comprises three bedrooms and two separate reception rooms. The property is in excellent condition throughout<br><br>Price £69,950. |
| **Third advertisement**<br>Appeals to gardeners | **South Facing Garden**<br>This three bedroom, two reception property is in first class condition throughout. A particular feature is the well stocked 60' south facing garden which has been lovingly tended by the present owners.<br><br>Price £69,950. |

## Setting an advertising budget

In Southern England, the cost of local property advertising is usually included in the agency fee. In Northern England many agents charge for all advertising and will want to agree an advertising budget with you at the time of instruction.

You should be aware that many agents make a profit from selling you advertising space and therefore have an incentive to sell you as much as possible. You should be cautious about agreeing to a major advertising campaign straight away. For most properties a budget that covers three or four local advertisements should be sufficient. If necessary, the budget can always be reviewed at a later date.

## National advertising

For most properties a local advertising campaign will be sufficient. However, some properties will benefit from further exposure in a Regional, National or Specialist publication. Such properties might include:

- High value properties
- Waterside properties
- Properties with equestrian facilities
- Properties that might have an appeal as a holiday home
- Highly unusual/individual properties
- Properties with potential for dual residential/commercial usage
- Properties with investment/lettings potential

If your property falls into one of these categories, you should ask your agent to advise you on the cost of an advertising campaign in the appropriate publications. The cost of such advertising is nearly always borne by the vendor, not the agent.

## Editorial coverage

Most local property newspapers have an editorial section which features a small number of properties each week. Most papers give each of the agents space in the editorial section on a rota basis. Editorials often generate far more enquiries for a property than an ordinary advertisement and it would be well worth trying to persuade your agent to include your property in their next editorial feature.

## Open house

A more unconventional approach to advertising is the open house. For some reason many purchasers are far more willing to attend an open house than to arrange a specific appointment to view a property. Perhaps they feel under less pressure. Perhaps they don't want to commit themselves to a precise time. Whatever the reason, advertising an open house can generate far more interest than a conventional advertisement.

The house is advertised as usual except that the times of the open house are prominently displayed. Some open house advertisements include the full address. In other cases the address is withheld so that the agent can take the applicant's details and verify them to be genuine prior to the appointment.

## Coming soon advertisements

A variation on the open house idea is the 'coming soon' advertisement. This is effectively a teaser campaign. Advertisements appear over a period of two to three weeks that say:

---

**Coming soon**

Four bedroom detached property in Lincoln's Fields area. The property is in need of some updating and refurbishment. Price guide £100,000.

---

Buyers who respond to the advertisement are all invited to view the property on a predetermined day at a predetermined time. No one is allowed to see the property until this time. The effect of several buyers arriving at once is that the property appears to be in great demand. As a result it is often possible to achieve a premium price.

# 14

# SHOWING PEOPLE AROUND

## WHO SHOULD CONDUCT THE VIEWINGS?

An estate agent will nearly always show a house more effectively than the owner could themselves. There are two reasons for this:

- Purchasers are more likely to tell the agent what they *really* think of a property. This feedback helps the agent to overcome objections.

- Experience will have taught the agent how to show each property to its best advantage.

You should therefore ask your agent to accompany as many viewings as possible, even if they are at a time when you will be at home yourself.

## PREPARING FOR A VIEWING

A well conducted viewing should aim to appeal to at least three of the five senses:

### Sight
- Try to ensure that the house is as tidy as possible.
- Draw all the curtains right back from the windows to make the rooms appear bigger and brighter.
- On dull days turn all the lights on – electric light is much warmer and more friendly than daylight (although sunlight is best of all).
- In spring, autumn or winter light a fire if you have one.

### Sound
- Turn the television off. It makes people feel that they are intruding.
- Put some background music on quietly (classical is best).

- Close the windows if the house is affected by any sort of background noise (traffic, trains, etc.).

### Smell

- Attractive smells can make a very positive impression – coffee brewing, bread baking, food cooking are all homely and atmospheric.
- Unpleasant smells can be very off-putting; these include dogs, tobacco, air fresheners and dirty bins.

### Atmosphere

I was once told a story about a beautiful flat that had failed to sell after more than a hundred viewings. Eventually the agent discovered that the reason was that the vendors (who were divorcing) were showing purchasers round in an atmosphere that was so poisonous that all they wanted to do was get out. By conducting viewings whilst the vendors were out the agent was able to obtain an offer within a few days.

### Dogs

A barking dog is for many people a most unpleasant first impression of the property. Try to take the dog out for a walk when a viewing is expected. If that is not possible, shut the dog in the car or in a back room until the potential purchasers have left.

## WHEN THE AGENT IS CONDUCTING THE VIEWING

### Your role

If the agent is conducting the viewing the best thing that you can do is to go out. If that is not possible, the next best thing is to stay out of the way (preferably in one of the less attractive rooms) until the agent has left. The agent will introduce you to the purchasers when they view the room that you are in but otherwise it is best for you to play no part in the proceedings.

## CONDUCTING A VIEWING YOURSELF

The following hints will help you to make the best of every viewing:

**Preparation** Ask the agent about the purchasers' background – their job, hobbies, etc. It is much easier to strike up a conversation with someone when you know something about them. Ask the agent also about the purchaser's main requirements (e.g. large garden, lots of space downstairs, low maintenance, etc.). This will enable you to stress these key points during the viewing.

## Greeting

First impressions really do count. Smile when you greet the purchasers – it can make a real difference.

## One of you or two

Only one of you should conduct the viewing. Your partner will only get in the way and make the rooms seem smaller.

## Order of rooms

Show the buyer the best room first. Take them round the rest of the house in a logical order then end up in the best room again at the end. This will mean that their first and last impression is a good one.

## After you

A room always seems bigger when it is empty. You should therefore always let purchasers enter each room first.

## Don't talk too much

Many vendors, perhaps through nervousness, point out every power point and dimmer switch. This can be most off-putting. It's really best to say as little as possible. You should, however:

- Relate the house to the purchaser's requirements e.g. I understand you wanted a big garden. This is 1¼ acres.

- Point out things the purchasers' might not notice themselves e.g. you could knock the pantry through to make a breakfast area here.

- Create a warm atmosphere by saying things like how happy you have been in the house.

## Privacy

Couples need time alone to discuss the house before they leave. The best way to achieve this is to send them out to look at the garden on their own.

## Security

These days you cannot be too careful. I was once told a story about a purchaser with several million pounds to spend, who was seen to steal a bottle of perfume during an accompanied viewing. Keep your eyes open and never leave purchasers alone.

## Handling questions

Be cautious about answering questions like 'Why are you moving?' It is so easy to put purchasers off.

## Dealing with rude people

You may meet someone who spends the whole visit being rude about your house. It really is best to ignore such comments unless the provocation is extreme. Some people are just rude by nature. Others may actually be interested in the property and might be trying to talk the price down.

## Handling offers

On no account should you get embroiled in price negotiations yourself. It is so easy to say something that you later regret. If a purchaser makes an offer, whatever it is, thank them enthusiastically and refer them to the agent.

## At the end of the viewing

However disinterested the purchasers appear, end the viewing by offering them a chance to go round again and/or to come back for a second look.

## Obtaining feedback

The agent should let you know what every purchaser thought within 48 hours of the viewing. If they do not, ring them.

## Prepare for disappointments

Purchasers are often quite nervous when they are viewing someone's house and some cover up this nervousness by saying how lovely everything is. This doesn't mean they want to buy it. Be prepared to find that many promising viewings do not result in an offer.

## Maintain your enthusiasm

No matter how many people you have shown round, it is vital to maintain your enthusiasm. I have know of many cases where houses have failed to sell because their owners (or agents) have grown sick of showing people around. If you do not seem interested in selling the property no purchaser will wish to buy it.

# 15

# THE FIRST REVIEW MEETING

Your house has been on the market for about four weeks (eight weeks in the north). It has been advertised, details have been sent out, and purchasers have been telephoned. You may well have had some viewings but there is still no sign of a buyer.

If this is the stage that you have reached, then it is time to visit your agent for a review meeting. Telephone your agent, tell him that you are concerned that the property has not yet sold and ask for an appointment to discuss what else can be done. Try not to get drawn into a discussion over the telephone. A review meeting really is something that needs to handled face to face.

## HAS THE PROPERTY BEEN PROPERLY MARKETED?

Start the review meeting by asking your agent, in a non-confrontational way, why he thinks that your property has not yet sold. Whatever answer he gives, you should ask him next to go through everything that he has already done to find a buyer. In particular you should ask about:

- **Feedback from existing viewings** – What comments have been made by the people who have viewed? Is there one thing that is putting people off? Could anything be done to change it?

- **Mail outs** – Ask how many sets of details have been sent out.

- **Phone outs** – Ask how many people have been telephoned to try to obtain a viewing. Ask what comments were made about the property by people who did not wish to view it. Again, is one thing putting people off? Could something be done to change it?

- **Other branches** – Check to ensure that any other local branches have details of your property.

- **Advertising** – Ask to see copies of all advertisements for your property. Are you satisfied these show your property to the best advantage?

- **Details** – Ask to see a copy of the details again. Are they still as well presented as the first set you saw.

## REVIEWING THE ASKING PRICE

The value of any property is ultimately determined by the price of the properties that are currently competing for the same buyers. The properties that are available change all the time and this means that the value of your property can fluctuate. If, for example, the house next door to you is put on the market for £5,000 less than yours, it will make it much more difficult to achieve your asking price. In order to check that your asking price is still realistic you should:

- Ask to see full details of all houses that the agent has sold in the same price range, whilst your property has been on the market. How do they compare to your own?

- Ask to see details of all other houses that the agent is currently marketing in the same price range. These properties will be competing directly with yours for the same buyers. How do they compare?

- Go through the current issue of the property newspaper with your agent. Are any of the properties advertised by other agents better value than your own?

In the light of such evidence you may need to consider reducing the asking price.

## WHAT ELSE CAN BE DONE TO FIND A BUYER?

If you are certain that the asking price is correct, you might ask your agent to take all or some of the following actions:

- Prepare new particulars. By taking new photographs and rewriting the particulars an old property can be made to seem like a new instruction. Sometimes this will result in viewings from people who were put off by something in the original particulars.

■ Ask the agent to send every member of his sales team to see your property. They may be more enthusiastic about selling a property that they have seen themselves.

■ Readvertise. Try to find a different aspect to feature – perhaps the garden, the history of the house, anything to make it appeal to a different group of purchasers.

■ Consider national or regional advertising. For many properties national advertising produces disappointing results. However, it might be worth considering one advert to test the market in a larger geographical area.

■ Increased incentive. Consider offering a bonus of say ½% to the individual negotiator who sells the property. This can transform their motivation! You will need the approval of the Branch Manager or Proprietor. (This was covered in more detail in Chapter 7.)

## CHANGING AGENTS

You may discover during the review meeting that your agent has not been doing his job effectively. If this is the case, you must tell him why you are dissatisfied. This is not a time to beat about the bush.

Four weeks is probably too soon to consider changing agents but, if you have good cause for dissatisfaction, it might be the best thing to do. However, before you disinstruct your agent, you should check carefully the terms of any sole agency agreement that you have signed. If you do not you could find yourself liable to pay two lots of agency fees. (This is covered in greater detail in Chapter 17).

# 16

# WHAT TO DO IF IT STILL WON'T SELL

Around eight weeks (sixteen in the North) have passed and there is still no sign of a buyer. What should be done next?

## ARRANGE A SECOND REVIEW MEETING

The first thing to do is to arrange a second review meeting with the estate agent. This should be conducted in a very similar way to the first one.

- Ask the agent why he thinks your property hasn't sold.

- Ask what comments have been made by people who have viewed – is one thing putting them off?

- Ask how many sets of details have been sent out.

- Ask how many people have been told about the house on the telephone.

- Ask what comments have been made by buyers who did not want to view, having seen the details. Is one thing putting them off?

- Check that the property has been circulated to any other local branches.

- Ask to see copies of advertising for the property run since the last review meeting.

- Ask to see a copy of the details again.

■ Ask the agent again if he will accompany all viewings if he is not already doing so.

■ Consider rewriting the details if you have not already done so.

■ Consider a For Sale board if you don't already have one.

■ Consider an open house, if you haven't already tried one (see Chapter 13).

■ Ask the agent to send every member of the sales team to view the house for themselves.

## REVIEWING THE ASKING PRICE

If the property has not sold after eight weeks it could well be that the asking price is too high. Try to assess this by:

■ Asking to see details of all other properties in the same price range as yours.

■ Asking to see details of properties that the agent has sold in the same price range since the last review meeting.

■ Looking at the price of any similar properties to your own that have been advertised in the newspaper.

Try to be honest with yourself and ask how your property compares to the competition.

## CHECKING UP ON YOUR AGENT

If you are certain that the asking price is realistic, the next thing to do is check up on how well your agent is marketing your property. This can be done in a number of ways:

■ Ask a friend to register with your agent as a buyer for a property like yours. What sort of service do they get? Is your property promoted both on the telephone and by the sending out of written particulars?

■ Ask your friend to arrange to actually view your property with your estate agent. How well do they feel that the property is being sold?

■ Phone the agent yourself to enquire about a property that has been advertised at a similar price to your own. Is your property also mentioned?

■   Phone the agent and say that you have seen the For Sale board outside your house. Does the agent really push hard to try to get a viewing?

If such tests reveal that your property is still being effectively marketed then there is no alternative but to be patient. If not the time may have come to change agents.

# 17

# DISINSTRUCTING AN ESTATE AGENT

The time may come when you have to accept that your first agent is not going to find a buyer within a reasonable period of time.

Once you reach this point, the first decision to make is whether to instruct a second agent as well as or instead of the first one.

## SOLE AGENCY *v.* MULTIPLE AGENCY

The pros and cons of sole versus multiple agency are explored in detail in Chapter 9. The main arguments are:

- Multiple agency encourages agents to work for themselves, not for you.

- Overexposure of the property can reduce the chances of finding a buyer.

- Multiple agency is more expensive.

- A sole agent has more incentive to work harder to achieve a sale.

For all these reasons the best course of action in most situations is to disinstruct the first agent and to appoint the new agent on a sole agency basis.

## HOW TO DISINSTRUCT AN AGENT

Disinstructing an agent is probably best done over the telephone. Thank the agent for his work in trying to find a buyer and tell him that you are sorry that he was not successful. Then tell him politely, but firmly, that you will now be instructing another agent and that you would like him to take the property off his books. You should expect the agent to try to persuade you to stick with him for a little longer and he may even offer incentives, such as extra advertising, to persuade you to do so. You should not be swayed.

## CONTRACTUAL OBLIGATIONS

Your sole agency agreement may impose contractual obligations on you and you should check it carefully before disinstructing your agent. Common obligations would be:

- **A notice period for disinstruction** (typically two weeks) may be required.

- **Withdrawal fee** Many agents, particularly in the North of England, will charge a withdrawal fee if they are disinstructed for any reason. This could be several hundred pounds.

- **Out-of-Pocket Expenses** Many agents, again particularly in the North of England, require reimbursement of all outstanding expenses such as advertising, colour photography, etc., at the time of disinstruction.

## BREAKING A SOLE AGENCY AGREEMENT

If you granted the agent a period of sole agency you will usually be contractually obliged to honour it. If the property is sold by another agent within the sole agency period you could find yourself liable to pay two agency fees. You might try to persuade the original agent to release you from the agency agreement by pointing out that he has nothing to gain from keeping a dissatisfied vendor on his books. However, the agent is not obliged to release you from the agreement early and if he will not, you have no choice but to delay instructing the new agent until after the original agreement has expired.

## AVOIDING COMMISSION DISPUTES

A fee will be payable to the first agent in the event that the property is sold to a buyer who has previously viewed it through that agent. To avoid arguments in the future it is as well to write to your agent to ask him to do two things:

- To confirm that he has taken the property off the market.

- To provide a list of the names of all purchasers who have viewed through him.

# 18

# INSTRUCTING A SECOND AGENT

## Choosing an agent

The most obvious agent to instruct the second time round will be the runner-up in your original beauty contest. However, this decision should not be an automatic one. If another agent has sold a lot of houses in your area during the time that yours has been on the market, then it would be well worth asking that agent to value your property before you make a final decision.

## Booking the appointment

All the local agents will know that your property has been on the market and there is nothing to gain from trying to hide this. However, it is important that the agent should not think that the appointment is a guaranteed instruction. If he does he may send a junior member of staff to take the details. To avoid this you should tell him on the phone that:

- You wish to instruct a new agent on a sole not a multiple agency basis.

- That you need advice on the asking price and would like to see details of similar properties in the same price range (both sold and available).

## Preparing for the appointment

You should prepare for the agent's visit in the same way as you would for any other viewing. Agents are human too, and their valuation will be affected by how well the property is presented.

### Establishing the ground rules

The agent will often expect an appointment at a house that is already on the market to be a guaranteed instruction. You should make it clear at the beginning of the appointment that this is not the case. Tell the agent that you are disappointed that the first company that you instructed did not find a buyer and that you are anxious not to make another mistake.

### The agent's sales presentation

Having agreed on an asking price, the next stage is to ask the agent what he will do differently from the first agent to market your property. In particular ask him:

- How he will present the particulars differently.
- How and where he will advertise.
- How many purchasers he has on his books.
- Why he thinks the house has not sold already.
- What other properties have recently sold in the same price range.

### Negotiating a fee

You will be in a weaker position to negotiate a fee than you were the last time around. The agent will know that your property has proved to be difficult to sell and will therefore quite probably hold out for a higher fee. However, this does not mean that you have to accept whatever fee is offered. The techniques outlined in Chapter 7 are well worth trying again. You might also suggest that you have an alternative agent in mind who you will instruct if an agreement cannot be reached.

### The sole agency contract

The precautions outlined in Chapter 10 should be taken before an agreement is signed. Again, don't be pressurised into signing an agreement on the spot. If you have any doubts ask the agent to leave the agreement with you.

### The sole agency period

The period of sole agency should be similar to the period given to the original agent – eight weeks would be typical. Any less and the agent will be reluctant to spend money marketing a property that he may not sell. Any more and you run the risk of being stuck with an ineffective agent.

### Instructing an agent on a multiple agency basis

There are circumstances where it is appropriate to instruct a second agent on a multiple basis. Perhaps the second agent is based in another town or suburb or advertises in a different newspaper. However, a third agent will very seldom do anything to increase your chances and a fourth or fifth may actually make it more difficult to find a buyer. However desperate you are to sell I would urge you not to overexpose the property.

## What to do if it still won't sell

If the property still won't sell, the only thing to do is to repeat the process outlined in Chapters 15 and 16. Hard as it is to accept, you have now done everything that can be done. If you are not willing or able to be patient, the only thing left to do is to begin reducing the asking price until you reach the figure at which the property sells immediately. Be warned, this could be many thousands of pounds less than its true value.

# 19

# GENERAL PRINCIPLES OF HANDLING AN OFFER

At last the moment you have been waiting for has arrived – you have received an offer. Unfortunately you cannot afford to breathe a sigh of relief just yet. A great deal of care will still be necessary in order to ensure that the best possible selling price is achieved and that the sale goes through to a successful completion. Three general principles will help to ensure that your negotiations have the very best chance of reaching a satisfactory conclusion.

## Don't handle negotiations yourself

Whatever the temptation, you should never handle negotiations yourself. Your estate agent will be able to negotiate an offer more effectively than you for a number of reasons.

- **Experience** – Your agent has the experience of having negotiated many other sales before.

- **Emotional involvement** – The agent should be able to negotiate in a calm and businesslike fashion without the burden of emotional involvement.

- **Extra thinking time** – Direct negotiations often mean that you are forced into giving an answer or making a concession on the spot. By negotiating through a third party, who does not have the authority to reach a binding agreement on your behalf, you buy invaluable thinking time.

An astute buyer will know that he will be better off by negotiating directly with the vendor and may try to apply considerable pressure in an attempt to persuade you not to involve the agent in the negotiations. You should not give in to such tactics. Doing so could cost you thousands of pounds.

## Don't take offence at low offers

Under the Estate Agents Act, an estate agent must inform you of every offer that he receives for your property immediately and in writing. Should you receive what you consider to be an insulting offer for your property, don't shoot the messenger. Your agent is only complying with his statutory duty.

The receipt of frequent low offers is also evidence that the agent is doing his job effectively by asking everyone who views the property if there is any price at which they would be interested in buying. This type of closing question does occasionally result in a sale to a purchaser who is embarrassed about making a low offer. Unfortunately, it also produces a number of low offers.

## Conduct negotiations in writing

Negotiations should be conducted in writing or by fax wherever possible. This will ensure that your position is not misrepresented and will save a lot of unnecessary arguments about exactly what was agreed later on.

# 20

# PREPARING TO NEGOTIATE

**IS YOUR PROSPECTIVE BUYER IN A POSITION TO PROCEED?**

Before you even begin to discuss the issue of price, it is vital to find out about your potential buyer's ability to proceed. Vital questions to ask include:

- The buyer's ideal time-scale.

- The reason for the move.

- Has the buyer got property to sell?

- If so, has that property been sold?

- If so, what stage has the sale reached?

- Are there any other dependent transactions in the chain?

- If so, exactly what stage has each transaction reached?

- Will the buyer require a mortgage?

- If so, what percentage of the purchase price will the mortgage be for?

- Which mortgage lender does the buyer intend to use?

You should be extremely wary about dealing with any buyer who cannot or will not answer these essential questions.

## WEIGHING UP THE OFFER

Whilst price will usually be the most important factor, speed and certainty will also be important to most sellers. An offer that is slow to complete could cost you an extra mortgage payment or might even result in you losing your purchase. You should also remember that an offer that falls through will, apart from the disappointment, also cost you a substantial amount of money in wasted legal and survey fees.

Factors that could prevent a buyer from completing his purchase quickly and smoothly might include:

### Length of chain

Every additional transaction in the chain increases the chances of something going wrong. You should be looking for someone with the shortest possible chain. Purchasers with nothing to sell are best of all.

### Size of mortgage required

A buyer who has applied for a high percentage mortgage (say 95% or more) may be unable to proceed if the property is downvalued on survey. Generally speaking buyers who need to borrow a lower percentage of the purchase price are more likely to complete. Cash buyers are the most likely to complete of all.

### Choice of lending source

Some lending sources are able to get most mortgage offers out within days. Others take weeks. Ask your estate agent if he has an opinion about the efficiency of the lending source that your buyer has chosen.

### Choice of solicitor

A solicitor who is inexperienced, pedantic, overworked or just inefficient can delay a sale for weeks. Ask your agent for his opinion of the firm that the buyer has chosen (see also Chapter 25).

All these factors should be carefully weighed up before you decide on what price you would be prepared to accept from the buyer.

## HANDLING AN OFFER FROM A BUYER
## WHO IS UNABLE TO PROCEED

On many occasions your enquiries will reveal that your would-be buyer is not yet in a position to proceed. Common reasons would be:

- The buyer is unlikely to be able to raise the money.
- The buyer has not yet found a buyer for his own property.
- The buyer has an incomplete chain.

There are very few circumstances where you have anything to gain from giving a commitment to sell your property to someone who is not yet in a position to buy it and the best advice is usually to refuse to even commence negotiations until the buyer is able to proceed. You should be warned that people can get very emotional about losing a house that they have set their heart on and some may try to persuade you to accept their offer by making all sorts of rash promises. Do not be swayed, most will amount to nothing.

When refusing an offer from an unproceedable buyer, the greatest care must be taken to remain on good terms with him. His buying position can and often does change overnight and you must do everything possible to ensure that it is easy for him to come back to you if and when he sells his own property.

## Sell the benefits of your position

A good buyer will be just as concerned as you to avoid the expense and disappointment of an abortive sale and the attractiveness of your position as a seller could well influence the price that the buyer is prepared to pay. If you are in a good position to sell, you should be sure to point this out when responding to an offer. Circumstances that may be attractive to a buyer would include:

- Able to move out immediately or at short notice if necessary.

- Short upward chain.

- Not buying another property.

- Already found a property to buy.

# 21

# NEGOTIATING THE PRICE

Your initial response should be in writing. It should follow this format:

(1) Thank the purchaser for his offer (regardless of how low it was).

(2) Summarise your understanding of the purchaser's buying position (this will help to avoid arguments later).

(3) Sell the benefits of your selling position.

(4) State the price that you would be prepared to accept.

(5) Give your detailed justification for how you arrived at this figure.

(6) Restate that you are keen to sell.

(7) Ask the buyer to make a revised offer.

Here is an example of such a letter:

Dear Mr Jones,

Re: 27 The Avenue, Anytown. Subject to contract.

[1]  Thank you for your offer for the above property of £90,000.

[2]  I understand that your buying position is as follows:

- You have sold your existing property to a first time buyer.

- Your own buyers have a mortgage offer and are pushing you to find somewhere.

- You will be arranging a mortgage for approximately 70% of the purchase price from the XYZ Building Society.

- You would like to exchange contracts in 6 - 8 weeks.

[3] I confirm that I am not buying another property immediately and that I would be prepared to move out of the house within 6 - 8 weeks.

[4] The price that I would be prepared to accept for the property is £97,000 and I believe that this is fully justified by the prices achieved for similar houses in the area. Relevant comparables include:

[5] - Number 37 which has no garage was recently sold for £95,000.

- Number 45 which is very similar to mine recently sold for £97,500.

[6] I believe that both the house and my selling position could suit you and your family very well and we would like to sell to you if a price can be agreed.

I look forward to hearing from you with a revised offer shortly,

Yours sincerely,

## NEGOTIATING TECHNIQUES

Few offers will be agreed in the first round. When conducting negotiations it is important to remember that both parties need to feel that they have won. If the other party is allowed to become entrenched in his position, it will become very much more difficult to achieve a satisfactory solution. There are many techniques that can be used to diffuse the hostility of a negotiation.

### Ask the purchaser to justify his offer

Almost every estate agent in the country can tell you a story about a sale that fell through because the two parties could not agree about the value of a garden shed, an old piece of carpet, a wooden toilet seat or something equally ridiculous.

The danger of conventional negotiation techniques is that they are highly confrontational. All too often such negotiations become deadlocked because both parties are too proud to concede another round. This is an emotional, not a rational, response but it could easily cost you a sale if you let it.

A much better way to negotiate is based on the simple principle of asking the other party to explain *how* he arrives at his offer. You might achieve this by writing a letter to him along these lines:

Dear Mr Jones,

Re: 27 The Avenue, Anytown. Subject to contract.

Thank you for your revised offer of £95,000. In my last letter I showed you how I arrived at my figure of £97,000 by reference to two comparable properties in the immediate area. I wondered if you would be kind enough to let me know *how* you arrived at your figure of £95,000.

I do hope that we will be able to reach an agreement and I look forward to hearing from you again soon.

Yours sincerely,

The buyer must respond with some sort of justification for the offer that he has made. This should ensure that future negotiations remain based on factual rather than emotional issues. This technique can be used again and again through subsequent rounds of the negotiations and can play an important role in preventing the negotiations from becoming deadlocked.

### Trade concession for concession

It can be very dangerous to ask the other party to concede something without giving something in return. You should always be on the look-out for an opportunity to trade a concession for a concession. For example:

- If you will pay an extra £1,000 I will agree to take the property off the market immediately.

It is important to realise that the value of the concession need not be equal to the value of what you are asking for in return.

### Offering non-financial concessions

A non-cash concession can often have a disproportionate value to the other party. For example, by moving out one day sooner you might be able to save your purchaser from paying a whole month's additional rent. It is therefore well worth trying to find out about any requirements of this nature that your buyer might have. These might include:

- Completion date

- Completion periods

- Exchange date

- Removal of the property from the market

- Fixtures and fittings

- Carpets and curtains

By making concessions in these areas you might well be able to avoid deadlock and/or secure a valuable negotiating advantage.

### Breaking deadlock

It is very frustrating to be unable to agree an offer for the sake of a relatively small amount of money. When the amount at stake is small it can be worth contacting some of the people higher up or down the chain to see if they are prepared to make a contribution. The vendor of a one million pound house at the top of the chain may be prepared to pay a few thousand pounds directly to someone lower down the chain in order to facilitate a move. It is usually best to leave it up to the agent to try to negotiate such a solution.

## Always leave the door open

It is surprising how often purchasers who make a low offer for a property early in their search, return to make an acceptable offer for the property days, weeks or even months later. For this reason it is vital to remain on good terms with everyone who makes an offer and to ensure that it is easy for them to reopen negotiations with you at any time in the future.

## CONSOLIDATION

Once an offer has been agreed, it is important to ensure that all the details are confirmed in writing as soon as possible.

It is also worth trying to arrange to meet your potential purchaser again. A meeting after negotiations have been successfully concluded can play an important role in consolidating the sale. There is no doubt that sales where a personal relationship has been established between the vendor and the purchaser are much more likely to complete.

# 22

# HANDLING MULTIPLE OFFERS

Occasionally a property will prove to be unexpectedly popular and two or more offers will be made by different purchasers within a short space of time. This can happen for a variety of reasons, one of which is that the property has been marketed at too low a price. If you suspect that this is the case go back to Chapter 3 and review the comparable evidence before you go any further.

Multiple offers must be handled with great care. It is all too easy to start off with two or three offers and to end up with none. The purpose of this chapter is to help you to avoid this.

## Look at the situation from the purchaser's point of view

Every potential purchaser who tries to buy your property and fails, will be left with a bill for legal and survey fees of several hundred pounds. Each potential purchaser will therefore need to be reassured at the outset that he will be treated fairly and that he has a realistic chance of getting the property. If your behaviour during early negotiations does not achieve this, some or even all of your potential purchasers will withdraw.

## Consider all the options

There are seven options for dealing with multiple offers:

(1) **A contract race** Two or more purchasers are told that whichever of them is able to exchange contracts on the property first will be allowed to buy it.

    *Advantages*        –  no risk to vendor

                                –  no need to choose between the parties

                                –  more than one chance of selling

*Disadvantages*    – even the suggestion of a contract race may cause both parties to withdraw

– losing party is left with legal fees to pay

(2) **Race to mortgage offer** Two or more purchasers are told that whoever gets their written mortgage offer first will be allowed to buy the property.

*Advantages*    – as above but abortive costs are lower to losing party

*Disadvantages*    – successful party can still withdraw after mortgage offer received

– losing party must still bear some abortive costs

– may result in neither party proceeding

(3) **Vendor funded contract race (or race to mortgage offer)** This works as in option one. However, the vendor agrees to pay the legal and survey costs of whichever party loses up to an agreed figure.

*Advantages*    – as option one but purchasers more likely to agree to participate if costs are underwritten

*Disadvantages*    – reimbursement of legal fees cannot make up for the disappointment of losing a property

– suggestion of race may still frighten off both parties

– cost to vendor will be several hundred pounds

(4) **Shut out agreement** A legal undertaking is given via the solicitors that one party will be given X weeks to exchange contracts without competition from any other buyer.

*Advantages*    – seller is protected against a sale dragging on for an unreasonable period

*Disadvantages*    –– seller is forced to choose between potential buyers at the outset

- seller gets no protection against buyer withdrawing

(5) **Sealed bids** Buyers are invited to submit their best and final offer in writing. The sealed bids are opened at a pre-agreed time and the highest offer wins.

| | |
|---|---|
| *Advantages* | - buyers can become excited by a sealed bid contest and overpay |
| | - system is seen to be fair to all potential buyers |
| *Disadvantages* | - system has no legal validity and has been discredited by previous unfair competitions in which the opening of the sealed bids has been followed by further rounds of negotiations |
| | - buyer who pays highest price may not be buyer who is most likely to proceed |
| | - a higher price might be obtained by open negotiations |

(6) **Open Negotiations** The agent continues to negotiate with each buyer openly until all but one have dropped out of the bidding.

| | |
|---|---|
| *Advantage* | - often the best way to obtain the highest price |
| | - purchasers' buying positions can be taken into account |
| *Disadvantages* | - negotiations can become acrimonious |
| | - successful buyer can withdraw at any time |

(7) **Remarketing the property** If you feel that the property has been undervalued the only option may be to remarket it. It will usually be necessary to leave a break of several weeks before the property is advertised again. You may also wish to change agents. This will cause considerable delays and when it is relaunched the initial impact will have been spoiled. For these reasons the decision to re-market a property should not be taken lightly.

## Deciding which option is best for you

Different options or combinations of options will appeal in different circumstances. If you are selling a highly desirable property in a buoyant market, a contract race may be worth considering. If you are selling an unattractive property during a recession a shut out agreement might be more appropriate. Whatever option you finally choose I would urge you to remember three things:

- Don't rush the decision.

- Take your estate agent's advice.

- Consider each buyer's position as well as the price offered.

# SECTION 3

# GETTING THE SALE THROUGH TO COMPLETION

# 25

# HOW TO CHOOSE A SOLICITOR

The right solicitor will be able to help you to avoid a great many of the common legal problems. When choosing a solicitor there are several important points to bear in mind.

## Choose a specialist

You need to choose a solicitor who specialises in residential conveyancing. This person is an expert in his field and will have come across all the common conveyancing problems before. This will help to ensure that your sale or purchase reaches a swift and trouble-free conclusion.

If you are using a small firm you should check to ensure that they deal with conveyancing on a regular basis. It is perfectly in order to ask them over the telephone how many conveyances they have dealt with during the last year.

## Instruct one solicitor not two

If you are buying a property, the second thing to check is that the solicitor that you have in mind is 'on the panel' (i.e. has been approved by your mortgage lender). In most cases the purchaser's solicitor will act for both the purchaser and the mortgage lender. However, if your solicitor is not on your mortgage lender's panel, they will insist on instructing a second solicitor to check your solicitor's work and safeguard their interests. This will inevitably mean unnecessary expense and delay. The question to ask before you instruct your solicitor is 'I will be obtaining a mortgage from the XYZ Building Society, are you on their panel?' If the answer is no, find another solicitor.

## Don't choose on price alone

Most solicitors these days will be prepared to give a fee quotation over the telephone. You will find however that conveyancing quotations vary enormously – a variation of 100% or more would not be uncommon. Whilst price is an important factor, it is very important not to select a solicitor on price alone. If a firm is able to quote a fee that is significantly below that of their competitors, then they will have to cut corners in their service somewhere in order to make a profit. In practice, this might mean that most of the actual work is done by an unqualified clerk rather than a partner, or that less time overall will be spent on each case. This might mean that your solicitor does not have time to answer telephone enquiries. The delays and frustration that can be caused by an overworked or inefficient solicitor will far outweigh the saving in the conveyancing fee.

### Get a recommendation

The best way to choose a solicitor is by recommendation. Ask your estate agent, friends and neighbours who have moved recently and your mortgage lender or broker for a recommendation. You will often find that the same firm is mentioned several times.

### When to instruct a solicitor

If you are selling a property there is a great deal to be said for instructing a solicitor at the time when you put the property onto the market rather than waiting until you have found a buyer. This will enable your solicitor to do some of the preparatory work such as obtaining the deeds in advance. This can save a lot of time once a buyer has been found.

### Handling your own conveyancing

It is perfectly possible to handle your own conveyancing. Several step by step DIY conveyancing guides have been published and the work involved is not actually all that time consuming or complicated. However the attitude of everyone else involved in the transaction – the estate agent, the other solicitor, the lending source, and your purchaser or vendor will be 'Oh no, they're not doing their own conveyancing'.

This hostile attitude can, on its own, cause considerable delays and my advice to most people therefore would be to leave conveyancing to the professionals.

# 26

# COMMON LEGAL PROBLEMS AND HOW TO OVERCOME THEM

The number of things that can go wrong with a sale are almost infinite and it would be impossible to cover them all in a single chapter. However, in my experience there are some problems that seem to come up time and time again. These include:

### Lost title deeds

The title deeds prove that you own your property. If the property is mortgaged they will almost certainly be held by your mortgage lender. If you own your property outright, the title deeds may be held by the solicitor who acted for you when you bought your property, by your bank or by a previous mortgage lender. On the other hand, they could have slipped down behind the radiator or have been thrown away by accident. If the title deeds to your property have been mislaid, you will need to prove again that you actually own the property. This may cause a considerable delay.

If you are selling a property, the best way to avoid such delays is to ask your solicitor to obtain the deeds at the time that you put your property onto the market, rather than waiting until a sale has been agreed.

### Disputes over the title

There are two systems of land conveyancing in England and Wales. In the registered system the title to the land is registered at the land registry and is guaranteed by the state. Disputes over title are therefore rare. In the unregistered system the title is not registered at all and must be proved by checking the details of previous conveyances. Where land is unregistered disputes over title are more common and negotiations can become quite protracted. One day all land will be registered. In the meanwhile if you find that the property that you are buying or selling is unregistered you should be prepared to allow extra time for the conveyancing process to be completed.

If you are selling a property, the best way to minimise any delay is again to instruct a solicitor at the time that you put the property onto the market.

## Delay in producing draft contract

These days most draft contracts comprise largely of standard or semi-standard phrases which are stored on a word processor. Unless there is something highly unusual about the property that is being sold, any delay in producing a draft contract is most likely to be caused by the inefficiency of the vendor's solicitors.

## Lost contract

If a contract is lost, a copy can usually be produced within minutes on a word processor. A lost contract should therefore not be accepted as a reason for a delay.

## Delay in obtaining office copy entries

Proof of title is supported by a copy, officially prepared by the land registry, of the entries on a land register. An office copy entry is divided into three sections. Section A confirms the address of the property, Section B confirms the quality of the title and Section C lists any charges or restrictive covenants.

The land registry is usually quite efficient and can be expected to provide office copy entries within 7 – 10 working days. The most common reason for delay is that the solicitor has not made an application for office copy entries soon enough.

## Restrictive covenants

A restrictive covenant is a promise not to use a property for certain specified purposes. Common examples would include:

- Not to use a property for any trade or business

- To keep the fences in good repair

- Not to build another house on the plot

Restrictive covenants can cause enormous problems and often cause delays in a sale.

The problems that covenants cause fall into two categories. In some cases, the existing property is in breach of an old covenant (e.g. a house has been converted into flats). In other cases the prospective purchaser wishes to do something that would break a covenant (e.g. build an extension or work from home).

Problems with covenants can be resolved in two ways. The first option is to track down the holder of the covenant and persuade him, or pay him, to release the property from it. However, in many cases this is not possible because his current address is not known or perhaps because he has long since died.

The alternative is to buy an insurance policy that covers the new owner against any loss that would be suffered in the event that the covenant is ever enforced. In most cases this is the quicker way to solve the problem.

## A caution

A caution is a warning placed on the Charges Register by a person who believes that he has an interest in a property which is not recorded. The most common caution would be placed by an estranged husband or wife who did not buy a property in joint names, but who still has an interest in it. The process for removing a caution involves writing to the Registrar. The Registrar has wide discretion to do what he thinks is appropriate. It may involve the payment of a sum of money to the person named in the caution or it may even involve a court case. The process of removing a caution can be quite protracted and may cause severe delays.

## Enquiries before contract

This is a list of questions sent by the purchaser's solicitor to the vendor's solicitor. The list is quite long and can appear to be quite daunting. However, in practice most of the questions are standard and many of the answers are 'I do not know' or 'rely on your own enquiries'.

Some questions do seem to cause a disproportionate number of problems, particularly:

* Arguments about boundaries and fences
* Arguments about sewers and drains
* Arguments about access roads and rights of way

Very often the best way to resolve such issues is to visit the property and discuss the problem directly with the other party. Very often a problem that could not be resolved in an exchange of three or four letters can be sorted out in five minutes face to face.

## Delays with local authority searches

The local authority search confirms amongst other things that the property has complied with all current building regulations, that no new property is to be built within fifty yards, and that no major road scheme is contemplated within two hundred yards. The mortgagor will not allow contracts to be exchanged until these enquiries have been answered. Unfortunately many local authorities have a considerable backlog of enquiries to deal with and a delay of up to two or three months is not uncommon in some areas. There are three ways to prevent a delay in obtaining a search from holding up your sale.

The best solution is to ask your solicitor to apply for a local authority search immediately that your property is put onto the market. The risk of this will be that the search will be out of date by the time a sale has been agreed.

If a sale had previously fallen through, another solution may be to try to buy the search from the solicitors that acted for the purchaser that did not proceed.

The final option is to do a personal search. You can literally do this yourself but most people retain a professional company to undertake the search on their behalf. If a mortgage is involved it will often be necessary to buy an insurance policy to warranty the purchaser against anything that has been missed by the person who undertook the search.

## Building regulation infringements

Many sales run into problems because an extension or other alteration has been completed without building regulation approval. In some cases it is possible to persuade the council to issue a certificate retrospectively. However the council may wish to make fairly extensive checks on the property before they are prepared to do this. In extreme cases it has proved impossible to sell a property until the offending alteration has been removed or demolished.

## Disputes over fixtures and fittings

The issue of which fixtures and fittings are to be included in the sale is one that often arouses considerable passions. The best way to ensure that such disputes do not hinder or jeopardise your sale is to ensure that a detailed list of the fixtures and fittings is recorded in writing and agreed at the time that the offer is accepted.

## Arguments over the deposit

Many solicitors advise their clients to accept a minimum deposit of 10%. This can cause real problems if the purchaser is applying for a 95% or 100%

mortgage. The main purpose of a deposit is to cover the vendor against any loss that he might incur in the event that the sale does not complete. Bearing in mind how rare it is for a sale to fall through between exchange of contracts and completion, you may decide to accept a reduced deposit of say 5%. The alternative is for the purchasers to borrow the money from their bank who may require a solicitor's undertaking to repay the loan once the mortgage funds have been released. It is as well to clarify your solicitor's attitude to this before the problem arises.

### Use of deposit by vendor

You may wish to use your purchaser's 10% deposit to fund the deposit that is required from your own vendor. Some solicitors have strong views about this and will not allow their client's deposit monies to be used in this way. It is therefore well worth establishing at an early stage whether you will be allowed to use your purchaser's deposit to fund your own purchase. If not, you will need a loan for this amount from your bank who may require an undertaking from your own solicitor to repay it from the proceeds of your sale.

### Dispute over completion dates

A completion date is usually set for 28 days after exchange of contracts. However, completion periods can be shortened to a few days; indeed it is even possible to do a simultaneous exchange and completion. Conversely the completion period can be lengthened. In some cases completions have been set for more than a year after exchange of contracts.

The more people there are involved in a chain the more difficult it is to find a completion date that is satisfactory to all parties. Again this is an issue that should be discussed in advance in order to avoid last minute problems.

## ADDITIONAL PROBLEMS WITH LEASEHOLD PROPERTIES

### Short lease

Many mortgage lenders will not lend on property where the lease has less than fifty years left to run. Many purchasers therefore are reluctant to buy a property with a lease of less than sixty years. Where a lease is shorter than this, it will often be necessary to negotiate a lease extension with the freeholder. This will almost certainly involve the payment of a fairly substantial sum of money and negotiations can become quite protracted. If you own a property with a lease of less than sixty years it is well worth making initial enquiries of your landlord as to the cost of a lease extension at the time that you first put your property onto the market.

## Defects with the lease

The purchaser's solicitor may claim to have found a defect in your lease. Sometimes the explanation is that the purchaser's solicitor is being pedantic. Sometimes the defect will be relatively minor and can be resolved through negotiation. On other occasions the defect will prove to be more serious. Some of the leases that were drawn up for the flats that were converted from large houses during the property boom of the 1980s were very carelessly worded. One of the worst examples that I heard of involved the owner of a first floor flat who did not have the right to walk from the road to his own front door. This was because the solicitor who drew up the lease had forgotten to give him the right to walk across a front garden that belonged to the ground floor flat. Where a defect in the lease is serious, it will need to be corrected by a Deed of Variation. This will require the freeholder's approval. The freeholder will almost certainly require that you bear the legal costs associated with drawing up a Deed of Variation and most freeholders will also require a payment for their inconvenience. Negotiations over a Deed of Variation can become quite protracted and the costs involved can be substantial. Where a defect in the lease is very serious, you may have a claim for negligence against the solicitor that handled the conveyancing for you when you bought the property.

## Unpaid service charges

Leasehold sales are often delayed because the vendor owes service charges to his freeholder. Even if such charges are in dispute, it will usually be necessary to pay them before contracts can be exchanged.

# 27

# WHAT TO DO WHEN THE SURVEY IS LATE

Often the first sign that a sale is not proceeding properly is a delay in arranging a survey appointment. Where the purchasers are seeking a mortgage, a survey will usually be arranged within two to three weeks of the offer being accepted. Where the purchasers are buying for cash, a structural survey should usually be arranged within one to two weeks. If a survey is not booked within these time-scales then you need to find out why.

## PROBLEMS WITH REFERENCES

A surprisingly high proportion of perfectly creditworthy people are refused a mortgage because they do not meet the mortgagor's strict lending criteria. Common problems include:

### Credit Scoring

Many lenders use a credit scoring process. This means that potential borrowers are given plus marks for some aspects of their lifestyle, for example being married with a family, and minus marks for others, such as having changed their job too frequently.

Whilst it may be statistically true that married borrowers are less likely to default on their mortgage payments, the credit scoring process is extremely arbitrary and it often leads to perfectly reputable and creditworthy applicants being refused a loan.

### Overtime and bonus payments

Many lenders will only allow half the value of overtime and bonus payments when calculating how much they will lend. Thus a civil servant on £20,000 p.a.

could borrow £60,000 whilst a salesman on £10,000 p.a. basic + £10,000 commission could only borrow £45,000. This can cause great confusion and delay. The problem can sometimes be overcome if the purchaser's employer will confirm in writing that the bonus payments are guaranteed, or if other evidence is available (such as bank statements) to show that the bonuses have been paid for a long time (say more than two years).

### Employer's reference

The lender will usually require a written reference from the borrower's employer. Employers are often very slow to comply with such requests. It is the purchaser's job to chase his employer to ensure that the mortgage application is not held up due to this.

### County court judgments for debt

A great many mortgage applications are refused because a routine credit search reveals that the borrower has a county court judgment for debt registered against him. Often a CCJ is evidence that a borrower is a bad credit risk, but in many instances it is evidence only of the rottenness of the system under which CCJs are recorded.

Anyone can seek to obtain a CCJ against anyone else by filling out a form which will be sent to the defendant's last known address. Many thousands of innocent people have CCJs registered against them because they did not know how to defend the action, or because the papers were sent to a previous address.

A further problem is that the search will include all CCJs registered at a given address, not just those recorded against the borrower personally. This means that credit is often denied because of a CCJ registered against an adult son or daughter, a divorced spouse, even a lodger who is living, or has previously lived, at the same address.

Despite the inadequacies of the present system, lenders will take the discovery of an undeclared CCJ extremely seriously and it will nearly always result in the mortgage application being refused.

Whilst problems with references will undoubtedly delay the progress of your sale, they need not prevent your buyer from proceeding. Many problems can be resolved by negotiation with the lender. Even if the first mortgage application is refused point blank, there is a good chance that a new application will be accepted by an alternative lender.

You can, however, only help to solve problems that you know about. Many purchasers are so embarrassed at being refused a mortgage that they tell the agent that they have changed their mind about buying the house without saying why. In such circumstances you are absolutely dependent on the skill and persistence of your agent to uncover the real reason for their change of heart, and if appropriate, to persuade the purchasers to reapply to an alternative lending source.

## INEFFICIENT LENDER

Sometimes the reason for the delay is just sheer inefficiency on behalf of the lender. Lending sources vary enormously in the time that it takes to turn round a straightforward mortgage application. Some are notoriously inefficient – your agent will know which they are. The only solution is to get your purchaser to chase his lender more frequently – every day if necessary until the required action is taken. In the most extreme case you might try to persuade the purchaser to withdraw his application and reapply to a more efficient lender.

## DELAYS CAUSED BY THE SURVEYOR

Sometimes your enquiries will reveal that the delay in carrying out the survey is the fault of the surveyor. Perhaps the surveyor is on holiday, perhaps he is in the middle of a particularly busy spell.

If you suspect this is the case you should ask the purchaser or the agent to ring the surveyor to ask either for a firm date for a survey, or for the return of the papers.

## SURVEY OPTIONS

Your purchaser will almost certainly commission one of three types of survey.

(a) **Mortgage valuation survey** This is the least comprehensive type of survey available. A typical report would be about two pages long. The purpose of this type of survey is to ensure that the property is satisfactory security for the mortgage that is advanced.

(b) **Home Buyer's Report** This is a much more comprehensive survey. It is intended to give the buyer a good idea about the condition of the property that is being purchased. It is prepared in a standard format in order to keep costs down. It will typically cost about twice as much as the mortgage valuation.

(c) **Full Structural Survey** This is the most comprehensive type of survey. It is prepared from scratch and will go into much more detail than the house buyer's report. It will typically cost about four times as much as the mortgage valuation.

It is clearly in your best interests to try to ensure that your property is surveyed in the least possible detail. The best way to achieve this is to have available your own recent structural survey (as recommended in Chapter 4). However, if a full structural survey is to take place you should try to ensure that it is combined with the mortgage valuation. Some buyers commission a basic mortgage valuation in the first instance then, once they have the result of this, commission a full structural survey. This is a more expensive way of doing things for the purchaser. Furthermore it can lead to unnecessary delays between the two survey reports.

# 28

# WHAT TO DO IF THE PROPERTY IS DOWNVALUED ON SURVEY

A great many sales fall through because the building society valuer downvalues the property on survey.

## WHY DOES IT HAPPEN?

The valuer is retained by the mortgage lender and his role is to ensure that the property is satisfactory security for the size of the loan that is to be advanced. Because he is retained by the lender, the surveyor will err on the side of caution when valuing a property. The consequence is that the mortgage valuation can often be 5 or 10% lower than the sale price that has been agreed.

## WHAT CAN BE DONE TO PRE-EMPT THE PROBLEM?

The best way to avoid the problems caused by a downvaluation is to prevent it from happening in the first place. There is a great deal that you can do to achieve this:

### Choose the lending source

Some banks and building societies have a reputation for using over-cautious valuers. Your estate agent will know which they are, locally. If your purchaser is intending to apply to one of these lending sources, you should ask your agent to try to dissuade them. The best way to do so is by telling them the true reasons for your concerns. If the property is downvalued your buyer will lose his survey fee and have to find another property. He should be as keen to avoid a down-valuation as you and he will often be prepared to reconsider his choice of lending source in order to do so.

### Choose the surveyor

Some building societies employ their own full-time salaried valuers but most still instruct an independent local surveyor. Each local surveyor will take a different view of property values and most towns have at least one who has a reputation for downvaluing. Your goal must be to prevent this surveyor from valuing your property. Your agent should be able to help you to achieve this by asking the purchaser or his mortgage broker to telephone the building society to request that the particular surveyor is not instructed. They will often comply with such a request.

### Prepare the house for the survey appointment

Surveyors are human too, and a well presented house will often be valued at a higher price than an untidy one. You should prepare for the surveyor's appointment in exactly the same way as you would prepare for any other viewing.

### Show the house to best advantage

The surveyor should be shown round the house in exactly the same way as any other purchaser. First impressions count for a lot and a local surveyor will probably have decided what value to put on the property within a few minutes of arrival.

Once you have shown the surveyor quickly around the house he will wish to be left alone to complete his detailed report. This might take anywhere between thirty minutes and four hours depending on the size of the property and the type of the report that is being prepared.

### Provide comparable evidence

The surveyor will value your property on the basis of the evidence of prices achieved for similar properties. One of the best ways to protect against a downvaluation is to give the surveyor your own selection of property particulars, chosen to support the sale price achieved for your property. This must be done tactfully. The surveyor will not respond well if he thinks that you are trying to tell him how to do his job.

## HANDLING A DOWNVALUATION

Whatever precautions you take, there is still a very good chance that your property will be downvalued by the surveyor. We will look next at what can be done to limit the damage.

## Get in first

Your estate agent will often be able to find out what figure the property has been valued at a day or two before the purchaser is told. This advance warning will enable the agent to present the bad news to the purchasers himself in the right way and can be an important factor in helping him to save the sale.

## The initial response

Most buyers will use a surveyor's downvaluation as an excuse to renegotiate the purchase price. You will wish to do everything possible to avoid this happening.

Your first response should be to defend your position. You might try three arguments:

- Explain that the surveyor's job is to act on behalf of the mortgage lender and that the valuation is therefore bound to be a cautious one.

- Point out that properties are often downvalued on survey. Ask your agent to back this up with some statistics.

- Remind the purchaser of the comparable evidence of other properties sold in the area which you used to justify the sale price that was agreed.

For the reasons outlined in Chapter 21 it is best to make this response via the agent and in writing.

## Subsequent negotiations

Any subsequent negotiations should be conducted in the same manner as I recommended in Chapter 21. The key principles are:

- Negotiate via the agent

- Negotiate in writing

- Use positional bargaining techniques to avoid deadlock

- Ask the purchaser to justify his revised offer

## WHAT TO DO IF NEGOTIATIONS BECOME DEADLOCKED

If agreement cannot be reached your buyer will walk away. Before you allow this to happen you must pause to consider whether taking all factors into account this will be in your best interests. Factors to consider might include:

■ Abortive legal costs

■ Wasted survey costs on your purchase

■ Loss of interest on the proceeds, if moving down market or not buying again

■ Chances of obtaining same purchase price from another buyer

■ Non-financial factors such as disappointment over the loss of your purchase.

Taking all these factors into account you will often find that the best course of action is to grit your teeth and accept the revised offer.

# 29

# WHAT TO DO IF THE SURVEY REVEALS THAT REPAIR WORK IS NECESSARY

As well as valuing cautiously, surveyors tend to take a pessimistic view about the extent and cost of any work that needs to be done to the property. The techniques outlined at the beginning of the last chapter will help to minimise such problems, but you must accept that the survey is likely to reveal at least one or two problems with the majority of properties.

### The purchaser's likely response

The purchaser is likely to seize upon any problem revealed by the survey as an opportunity to renegotiate the purchase price. His opening position is likely to be that the full cost of the repairs should be deducted from the purchase price. You will need to work hard to defend your position.

### Ask to see the survey report

Before you commence negotiations you should ask for a copy of the survey report. It is in your purchaser's interests to exaggerate the cost and extent of the works that are necessary and purchasers have even been known to invent problems not mentioned by the surveyor in order to try to get a price reduction. You should be very suspicious of a buyer who will not let you see the report. My instinctive reaction would be to refuse to commence negotiations without first seeing a copy of the survey report.

### Interpreting the surveyor's report

Dependent upon the urgency of the work, a surveyor will make one of the following recommendations:

- He can point out the fault and *recommend* that it is attended to.

- He can ask for a *formal undertaking* from the purchasers to carry out the necessary repairs within a certain time.

- He can insist that an expert is called in to investigate the extent of the problem and to assess the likely cost of rectifying it.

- He can recommend that the mortgage advance be made subject to a *retention*, that is to say that £X000 will be deducted from the mortgage advance and not released until the necessary work has been completed.

- He can recommend that the mortgage should be refused altogether.

### Your initial response

Your initial response should be to refuse to renegotiate the price. You might try to defend your position using some of the following arguments:

- The surveyor has been pedantic, the work is not necessary at all.

- The work is of a cosmetic nature. The purchaser did not need a surveyor to point out that the kitchen and bathroom need updating and that the property is in need of redecoration.

- The condition of the property has already been allowed for in the price agreed.

- The other properties recently sold in the area were in a comparable condition.

- The defects mentioned must be seen as fair wear and tear in a property of this age.

### Limiting the damage

If renegotiation seems inevitable, there is quite a lot that you can do to limit the damage.

**Get your own estimate** The surveyor's estimate of the cost of necessary work is likely to be at the top end of the scale. It can be well worth asking a contractor to give an accurate estimate of the cost involved. It could prove to be a lot less than the surveyor thinks.

**Offer to carry out the work yourself** Very often the buyer has absolutely no intention of carrying out the work that his surveyor has recommended. He is just using the report to get a price reduction. If you suspect that this is the case, you might counter it by offering to do the work yourself between exchange of contracts and completion.

**Offer a proportion of the cost** If the sale were to fall through at this stage, both parties would stand to lose a great deal. Having got so far, your buyer will wish to complete the purchase if at all possible and may well be prepared to settle for a price concession that represents only a small percentage of the cost of the works.

### Dealing with a very adverse survey

A very adverse survey report would be defined as one where the mortgage advance is refused altogether or where a mortgage offer is made subject to a retention of more than 20% of the property's value. By far the most common reason for such a result is subsidence.

It is unlikely that you will be able to negotiate your way out of a situation like this and it is almost inevitable that you will lose your purchaser and experience considerable delays before the property can be sold again.

The action you take might include:

■ **Commissioning your own structural survey** Just occasionally a second surveyor will not consider the problem to be serious.

■ **Commissioning a specialist structural engineer's report** Surveyors have a tendency to spot a crack and assume that a property is about to fall down. A structural engineer's report might prove that the problem is not as severe as it looks.

■ **Making an insurance claim** The cost of rectifying such serious defects will usually be covered by your buildings insurance.

### What to do if negotiations become deadlocked

If negotiations reach deadlock, the best advice would be don't panic and don't give the property away. It is surprising how often a second survey reveals none of the problems mentioned in the first.

# 30

# GAZUMPING, GAZUNDERING AND OTHER SUCH PROBLEMS

## GAZUMPING

The practice of gazumping arouses fierce passions. It happens when the vendor agrees a sale for his property and then subsequently accepts a higher offer from another party. It can happen at any time during the sales process, from five minutes after the first offer was accepted right up to the day that exchange of contracts was due to take place.

### Whose fault is it?

Gazumping is caused by human greed, not by estate agents. An estate agent's professional and legal duty is to carry out the instructions of his client. If his client instructs him to continue marketing a property after an offer has been accepted, then he must do so. If a second offer is subsequently received, it is the agent's legal duty to pass the offer on to the vendor. It is entirely up to the vendor to decide whether to accept or refuse the higher price.

### What you must do before you decide

If you receive a higher offer after you have agreed a sale, you need to proceed very carefully. It is all too easy to start with two offers and end up with none at all.

### Check out the second buyer's position

Before you do anything you must check out that the second buyer is in a position to proceed (see Chapter 20). Having checked out his position, compare it with the current position of your original buyer. At one extreme there would be nothing to gain from accepting an offer that was only marginally higher from a purchaser who has not yet sold his own property. At the other extreme it would be much harder to turn down a higher offer from a cash buyer the day after your original purchaser has lost the buyer for his own property.

### Assess the value of all other factors

You must also be sure to weigh up the value of all other relevant factors in the equation. These might include:

- **Timescale** How quickly could the second purchaser complete? Would this delay cost you money (e.g. in extra mortgage payments)?

- **Fairness of price** Is your property really worth the high price? If it is not the second sale may well not complete due to a downvaluation on survey.

- **Risk of losing your purchase** Would the delay caused by switching buyers jeopardise your own purchase?

### Consider all the options

There are many alternative ways in which you can use a second offer to your advantage. The options include:

- Accept the second offer and tell the original buyer they have lost the property.

- Inform the original buyers that you have received a higher offer from another party and invite them to match it. (This might go more than one round before a new price is finally agreed.)

- Invite both parties to compete in a contract race for the property. (See Chapter 22); (benefit: quicker completion.)

- Inform the original buyers that you have received a second offer. Tell them that you will not accept it provided that they exchange contracts before a certain date. (Benefit: quicker completion.)

- Inform the original buyer that you have received a second offer which you will not accept because you have agreed to sell it to them. (Benefit: consolidates relationship with original buyer but implies that competition is on the horizon.)

- Refuse second offer, don't tell the original buyer that you received one (This is sometimes the best way to deal with a nervous buyer.)

## Moral and ethical considerations

This section would not be complete without a few words about the effects of gazumping on the purchaser. If you do accept a second offer, the original buyers will be left with a substantial bill for abortive survey fees and legal costs in addition to the disappointment of having lost the property that they had set their hearts on. It is not my place to attempt to define the limits of moral behaviour, but I would ask that you should at least pause to consider the consequences of your actions, before you make your final decision.

## GAZUNDERING

When the market is poor gazundering is a common problem. A vendor is 'gazundered' when the buyer reduces his offer, without good reason, shortly before exchange of contract is due to take place.

The buyer who tries this tactic is banking on the fact that the financial and emotional costs to you of pulling out of the sale at such a late stage, will exceed the value of the reduction that he has asked for. When the property market is poor, buyers often get away with it. The following suggestion will help you to limit the damage if your purchaser tries to gazunder you.

**Negotiate via the agent** You will probably be very angry with the buyer for trying to gazunder you and this anger will seriously reduce your ability to negotiate effectively. Further negotiations really must therefore be conducted via the estate agent.

**Ask for reasons** Ask the buyer why he has reduced his offer at such a late stage. The buyer's embarrassment about the situation will be increased if he is forced to admit that he has no reason to ask for a price reduction and that he's just trying it on.

**Rejustify the price** Use comparable evidence to justify that the property is worth the original price that was agreed.

## The final decision

If these tactics don't work you will be forced to make a decision about whether to accept the reduced offer. It is all too easy to allow anger and emotion to get in the way of making the right decision. Before you tell your purchaser to go to hell, be sure to weigh up the financial value of factors such as:

■  Extra mortgage payments whilst the property is remarketed

■  The financial and emotional cost of losing your purchase

- Your realistic chances of obtaining the same price again from another purchaser

If you have a reserve buyer waiting in the wings you might be in a position to call your purchaser's bluff but on many other occasions the best thing to do is to bite your lip and accept the lower offer.

## Dealing with the consequences

There are two things that you might wish to do to claw back some of the money that you have had to concede to your purchaser.

**Gazunder your own vendor** Telephone the agent that you are buying through, explain the you have been gazundered and say that you fear that you will not now be able to complete your purchase at the original price agreed. This is a high-risk strategy. You may lose your purchase altogether, but if market conditions are so bad that you felt compelled to accept a lower offer, then your vendor might be forced to do the same.

**Remove fixtures and fittings** If all else has failed you might consider getting your own back by removing all fixtures and fittings not included in the contract. These might include things such as extra security locks, bathroom fitments, shelves, light fittings, plants, etc. The collective value of these fittings can often run to many hundreds or even thousands of pounds.

## WHAT TO DO IF THE BUYER WITHDRAWS

### Try to establish the reason

My experience is that once a buyer says that he wishes to withdraw from the purchase he usually does so. However, before you completely give up on your purchaser, it is worth double checking to make sure that you know the real reason for his change of heart. It is surprisingly common to find that there are problems that you don't know about which might be solvable. For example your buyer might have been refused a mortgage and be too embarrassed to tell the agent this. Instead he just says that he has changed his mind. If the agent can find out the truth, he might be able to help him to obtain a loan from another lending source.

### Don't despair

However disappointed you are, try not to despair. Your property sold once and it will sell again, you just need to be patient.

## Don't proceed with your purchase

Unless you are extremely wealthy, you should not even think about continuing with your purchase until you have found a buyer for your own property. One of the saddest cases that I dealt with as an agent involved a family who took out a ruinously expensive bridging loan to buy their dream home, failed to sell their previous home and ended up having both repossessed by the mortgage lenders. It could easily happen to you. However perfect your dream home is there will always be another.

# 31

# PROBLEMS WITH THE CHAIN

All the problems that I have covered in this third section can also occur with other sales up or down the chain. If you suspect that your own sale is being jeopardised or delayed by the inexperience or pigheadedness of other buyers and sellers in the chain, you may need to take matters into your own hands.

### Establishing what the problem is

It can be surprisingly difficult to find out the real cause of the delay. As in the game of Chinese whispers, information tends to be distorted when it is passed through the many parties involved in the chain. Furthermore, once tempers have become frayed, many parties seem to become more interested in whose fault it is that the chain is being held up, than in finding a way in which the problem can be resolved. You will need to work hard to cut through such nonsense.

### Start with your estate agent

It is your agent's job to know what is happening up and down the chain and he should certainly have an opinion as to what is causing the delay. However, no matter how convincing his explanation sounds, don't take his word for it. Ask him to contact all the other agents up and down the chain in order to establish the up-to-date position with each sale from first-hand sources.

### Checking a chain via the solicitors

If you are still not satisfied with the answers you are getting, a second option is to try to track the sale through the solicitors. Conveyancing solicitors habitually blame the other side for all delays, so ignore any such allegations and concentrate your questions on establishing where the problems lie and whether there is anything that you can do to expedite matters.

Start by asking your solicitor for his opinion as to where the problem lies. You might then consider checking this by phoning some or all of the solicitors in the chain. They are under no obligation to talk to you, and some will refuse to do so, but most will give you five minutes at least which should be ample time for you to achieve your purpose.

### Checking discreetly with other vendors

A final option is to try to speak directly to all the other parties in the chain. Each vendor will almost certainly be able to give you a telephone number for his own purchaser and in this way it should be possible for you to speak personally to everyone involved.

You will probably be surprised by the number of contradictory stories that you hear from different parties. The only safe way to be sure that you have established the real problem is to obtain information from several different sources so that you may cross check its accuracy.

### Late survey/mortgage denied

If a buyer further down the chain is having problems obtaining a mortgage then there is a great deal that you might be able to do to help. Re-read Chapter 27. Better still send them a copy of this book open at the relevant page!

### Inefficient solicitors

A less informed buyer in the chain might have instructed a solicitor who is inexperienced, overworked, lazy, pedantic, or just downright bloody-minded.

The best person to help you to overcome the shortcomings of another solicitor in the chain is your own solicitor. If you are faced with this situation you should ring your own solicitor and share your concerns with him. In return for payment for the extra time involved he might be able to guide, cajole or bully the other solicitor into doing the job that he is being paid for.

### Downvaluation on survey or gazundering

The recommendations made in the last chapter may help to diffuse the situation. If negotiations have already reached deadlock you might consider trying **three** last things.

**Offer to mediate** You might offer to act as a mediator for one final round of negotiation. If previous negotiations have been handled clumsily, you might still be able to snatch victory from the jaws of defeat.

**'Pass the hat up the chain'** Other parties in the chain might be prepared to contribute a sum of money to resolve a problem. This will often cost you less than the cost of an abortive sale. This hypothetical example shows a situation when such an offer benefits all parties:

Property 1 sale price £50,000
Property 2 sale price £100,000
Property 3 sale price £150,000
Property 4 sale price £250,000
Property 5 sale price £500,000 (vendors moving into newly built retirement home)

A downvaluation of 10% on Property 1 would leave the buyers £5,000 short of the funds needed to complete. To a first time buyer this would be a great deal of money. The vendors of Property 1 could not afford to concede £5,000 and the sale would fall through. However, the vendor of Property 5 could easily afford to fund the £5,000 shortfall, and it might well be in his best financial interests to do so. £5,000 represents approximately two months' loss of interest on the proceeds or one month's interest on a £500,000 mortgage.

An alternative solution might be for the vendors of Properties 3, 4 and 5 to agree to contribute £1,000, £1,000 and £3,000 respectively. This would represent approximately one month's extra mortgage for each of them.

It is surprising how often an insoluble problem can be overcome by passing the hat up the chain this way. All that is needed is someone with the knowledge and determination to negotiate it. In the absence of a better offer that someone will have to be you.

As an absolute last resort you might even consider offering to pay the disputed sum yourself either alone or in conjunction with other parties in the chain.

# 32

# WHAT TO DO IF THE CHAIN BREAKS DOWN

The suggestions given in the last chapter may help you to save a sale at the eleventh hour but realistically you must accept that in many cases you will be unsuccessful.

If the chain does break down, there are two last things that you might try to save the day.

### Subsidise a sale lower down the chain

This is essentially a variation on passing the hat down the chain. Consider this example.

Property 1 was sold at £50,000 to first time buyer
Property 2 was sold at £100,000
Property 3 was sold at £150,000
Property 4 was sold at £250,000
Property 5 was sold at £500,000 (The vendor was elderly and was not buying another property.)

Two days before contracts were due to be exchanged the buyer of the £50,000 property withdrew for no reason. The solution which was agreed worked as follows:

Each vendor contributed 1% of their sale price to a communal fund thus:

| Vendor 1 contributed | £    500 |
| Vendor 2 contributed | £1,000 |
| Vendor 3 contributed | £1,500 |
| Vendor 4 contributed | £2,500 |
| Vendor 5 contributed | £5,000 |
| | ———— |
| Total | £10,000 |
| | ———— |

This money was used to subsidise the selling price of the £50,000 property. Thus it was put back on the market at the bargain price of £40,000. As a result it sold within hours and the chain was saved.

Sadly solutions like this rarely work because the parties let their emotions get in the way of finding a solution or because no one available has the skill, patience, motivation and tenacity to negotiate a solution that is acceptable to everybody.

## Consider a part exchange

One last extreme solution to consider, if all else failed, is to offer to buy the property that is holding up your sale as a part exchange. If you have the funds available it is not as daft an idea as it sounds. Reconsider our previous example. The vendor of a property selling at £500,000 and not buying again would stand to lose a lot from a delay of three to four months whilst his property is remarketed. At say 6% p.a. loss of interest alone comes to £2,500 per month. It might well pay a person in this position to buy a cheap property in part exchange in order to expedite his own sale. Loss of interest on a £50,000 flat would, after all, be only £250 per month. The cost of buying and reselling the flat would be around £2,000. It is easy to see how the vendor could be better off. You should at least check the sums relating to your own position on the back of an envelope before you dismiss the idea out of hand.

## PROBLEMS UP THE CHAIN

All the things that could go wrong further down the chain can also go wrong with transactions further up it. However, there is one further factor to consider if you have lost or are at risk of losing your purchase and that is should you still complete on your own sale? The arguments for and against doing so are often finely balanced. Facts to consider include:

- **State of the market** If you are moving to a more expensive property in a buoyant market there is a risk that prices will continue to rise whilst you are out of the market. If the market is depressed you may be able to buy the next property for less than you had anticipated.

- **Improved negotiating position** Without a property to sell you will be in a much stronger buying position. This may enable you to negotiate to buy your next property at a much better price.

- **Cost of storage and removals** The cost of removals to and from your temporary address and/or storage charges will be quite significant.

- **Non-financial factors** Moving house is extremely disruptive. You must be sure to include the emotional cost of an extra move on both yourself and your family.

Taking all these factors into account it is probably not surprising that most vendors who lose their purchase would rather run the risk of losing their own buyer than face a double move.

# 33

# EXCHANGE OF CONTRACTS AND COMPLETION

## PREPARING FOR EXCHANGE OF CONTRACTS

You will know that you are nearly there when your solicitor asks you to arrange an appointment to sign the contracts. Although this is certainly a good sign, you would be well advised not to relax just yet. Things can and do go wrong at the very last minute. Two problems in particular seem to occur more often than most.

### Gazundering

The unscrupulous buyer knows that the later he leaves his attempt to gazunder you the more likely he is to succeed.

An attempt on the very day that contracts were due to take place is quite common. The advice given in Chapter 30 still applies, but the buyer knows that at this late stage you are less likely to walk away from the prospect of an immediate sale and he is likely to press home his advantage quite mercilessly.

### Arguments over completion dates

The longer the chain, the more difficult it will be to agree on a completion date that is acceptable to all parties. Sales have been known to break down on this point alone.

If a dispute over completion date is jeopardising your sale you should consider:

- **Negotiating a shorter or longer completion period** The conventional completion period is 28 days but there is no reason why it has to be. A completion period can be any length that is acceptable to both parties – a day, a week, a month, even a year; it is even possible to exchange contracts and complete simultaneously. Very short completion periods, say seven days or less, may involve your solicitor in extra work but the cost of this will be a great deal less than the cost of an abortive sale.

- **Agreeing to an uncoordinated completion date** If all else fails you might have to choose between moving twice or not at all. An uncoordinated completion means that you agree to vacate your property on a certain date in the knowledge that you will not get possession of your new property until, say, seven days later. The cost to you is the inconvenience of moving twice, extra removal and storage charges and probably the cost of a week's hotel accommodation. If the only alternative is an abortive sale, the cost could be justifiable.

## PREPARING FOR COMPLETION

At long last the moment you have been waiting for arrives and your solicitor telephones to tell you that exchange of contracts has taken place. You really are nearly home and dry now and a celebration is entirely in order. Nevertheless, it is still not too late for things to go wrong.

### Failure to complete

It is very, very rare for a sale not to complete at all. I have dealt with only three cases. In the first one the purchasers decided to end their marriage a few days before completion was due to take place. Neither party wanted the house and they ended up forfeiting their 10% deposit. In the second case the purchaser's father-in-law refused to honour a promise he had made to lend money to fund the purchase after a family row. Again the 10% deposit was forfeited. In the third, the vendor went insane between exchange and completion. The matter was referred to the court of protection who took over a year to complete the sale!

### REMOVAL ARRANGEMENTS

### Choosing a removal firm

All removal firms are not the same. The cost of making the wrong choice could be the loss of furnishings and ornaments that have taken a lifetime to collect. The best way to choose a removal firm is by personal recommendation. Ask your friends and colleagues if they can recommend a good one. Always get more than one quotation and be sure to base the final decision on reputation as well as on price.

### Removals only versus full packing service

Most removal firms offer a variety of service levels, ranging from a full packing service where they will literally do everything, to a basic service where they provide only the lorry and a single working driver. You will need to think carefully about the service that you need and be sure that the quotations that you get from different firms are all for the same level of service.

### Insurance

Many otherwise reputable removal firms limit their maximum liability for loss or damage to an absurdly low amount, sometimes just a few pounds per item. There are two ways to get round this problem. The first is to arrange for the necessary additional cover through your own household insurer. The second is to find another removal firm.

Perhaps if more people did the latter the removals industry would be forced to start making proper arrangements for the protection of its customers.

### Moving yourself

Moving yourself is hard work and it may not save you as much money as you think. Once you add up the cost of van hire and the hire of the chests or specialist removal cartons (without which things will get broken) you may well decide that the saving is not worth it.

If you do decide to got it alone, these tips will help things to go smoothly.

- **Van hire** Go to a large specialist depot. Many do an all-in removals package which includes van, carton and trolley hire. Remember that they will need to see your driving licence on the day of hiring.

- **Van size** If in doubt get the larger one. A larger van will allow more careful packing and reduce breakages.

- **Allow plenty of time** It will always take you longer than you think to move house – start early.

- **Anticipate making more than one journey** The contents of an average three bedroom house often do not fit into a 7.5 tonne box van (which is the largest that you can hire without an HGV licence). Allow time for a second or third journey.

## UTILITIES

### Arrangements for the new house

Unless you want to move into your new home by torchlight, arrangements must be made well in advance.

**Gas/Electricity/Water** Phone the new gas, electricity and water companies. Tell them that you are taking over the supply and that you do not want the service to be discontinued. Ask for written confirmation. Be sure to read the meters as soon as you arrive at the new property.

**Telephone** If your new property has the same exchange code, you will have the option of keeping your old phone number. If not you will usually be given a choice between taking over your vendor's old number or having a new one. Make sure of your arrangements well in advance and ask for written confirmation.

### Arrangements for the old house

Be sure to contact all the utilities to inform them that you are moving. Ask for a final account to be sent to your new address. Don't forget to read the meters before you go.

**Mail** The Post Office offers an excellent mail forwarding service at a very reasonable cost. It is well worth purchasing this service for at least a year in order to ensure that important post doesn't go astray.

## COMPLETION DAY

Such is the perversity of the house buying process that things can go wrong even on completion day itself. Although such problems are fairly rare, it is important to keep in touch with your solicitor throughout the day. Three specific problems are worth mentioning:

### Arguments over the release of keys

Your purchasers may ask if they can have the keys to your property before completion has taken place. You must never allow this, no matter what the circumstances, until your solicitor authorises it. This might be easier said than done when the purchasers are sitting on your doorstep with their removal men clocking up an overtime bill, but refuse you must. In the unlikely event of the completion not taking place the most terrible complications could arise if the buyers are already in possession.

## Delay in receiving the money

The money to fund the purchase of each property in the chain will almost certainly be sent by telegraphic transfer. In this age of satellite communications you might think that money could be transferred between banks instantly. You would be wrong. The system is terribly inefficient. It often takes several hours for funds to be transferred. What is more there is a shut-off time (usually 1.00 p.m.) after which any funds sent will probably not arrive until the next day.

Due to the inadequacies of the system, the non-arrival of the completion monies is a fairly common problem. If you do not receive the money for your sale you will not be able to complete on your purchase, indeed completion for the whole chain could be delayed until the next day. The inconvenience, cost and legal implications of this delay can be horrendous. Every purchaser in the chain will be contractually obliged to complete by a certain time of day (usually 1.00 p.m.). Should they not do so they will be legally liable for any extra expenses incurred by their vendor. The result can be a lawyer's field day with everyone blaming everyone else for the delay.

Unfortunately there is not much that you can do to avoid this problem although it is worth phoning your solicitor at around 12.00 midday to check that everything is OK. If there is a problem you will have at least an hour to solve it.

## ON ARRIVAL AT THE NEW HOUSE

Congratulations. You have done it – but before you completely relax it is worth doing two last things.

- **Test the services** Check immediately that you have gas, electricity, water and a telephone. If any of these services have been disconnected you will need to get onto the suppliers immediately.

- **Read the meters** It is all too easy to get caught for the previous owner's bill. Check the meters and make a careful note of the readings as soon as you move in.

- **Check the fixtures and fittings list** Check to make sure that all fixtures and fittings that should have been left have been. If something major has been taken in defiance of the contracted agreement you can threaten to sue for its return.

## THE LAST WORD

Moving house will never be easy, but I hope that this book has HELPED you to avoid some of the common pitfalls. All that remains now is to enjoy your new home.

And this book. Well, this book might serve one last useful purpose. I would suggest that you put it on a bookshelf in a prominent position so that if, at any time in the future, you find yourself thinking – wouldn't it be nice to have an extra bedroom – you can look at the cover and ask yourself – is it really worth it?

# USEFUL NAMES AND ADDRESSES

**British Association of Removers**
279 Grays Inn Road
London WC2 8SY          0171 837 3088


**The Incorporated Society of Valuers and Auctioneers**
3 Cadugan Gate
London SW1 X01S          0171 235 2282


**The Law Society**
113 Chancery Lane
London WC2A 1EL          0171 242 1222


**The Law Society of Scotland**
PO Box 75
26 Drumsheugh Gardens
Edinburgh EH3 7YR          0131 226 7411


**National Association of Conveyancers**
2–4 Chichester Rents
Chancery Lane
London WC2A 1EG          0171 405 8582


**The National Association of Estate Agents**
Arbon House
21 Jury Street
Warwick CV34 4EH          01926 496800


**The Royal Institution of Chartered Surveyors**
12 Great George Street
Parliament Square
London SW1 P3AD          0171 222 7000

# APPENDIX 1

## SAMPLE SOLE AGENCY AGREEMENT

## SAMPLE SOLE AGENCY AGREEMENT

# PALMER SNELL.
## Standard Terms and Conditions

**INTRODUCTION**

This document sets out the terms and conditions under which Palmer Snell will act for you in the sale of your property.

If you wish to instruct us, our Instruction Agreement is to be found opposite. When completed, it should be signed both by you (or a person acting on your behalf) as "Seller" and by a representative of Palmer Snell.

Additional specific items may be set out in greater detail in an accompanying letter which the Seller is requested to sign and return as acceptance of such items.

**CHOOSING THE RIGHT AGENT**

This is without doubt the most important decision that you will need to make.

At Palmer Snell we believe that there is only one choice. The majority of our instructions come from satisfied clients who have used our services previously and through recommendations.

Having successfully sold properties since 1811, there is hardly a problem that we have not encountered and solved. This is due to our experienced and fully trained residential sales teams located in every office throughout the area. Our high profile offices, backed by extensive local and regional advertising, set us apart from the rest.

YOU CAN INSTRUCT US ON ANY OF THE FOLLOWING TERMS:-

**1. SOLE AGENCY**

Commission of     % of the Agreed sale price plus VAT.

You will be liable to pay remuneration to us, in addition to any other costs or charges agreed, if at any time unconditional contracts for the sale of the property are exchanged-

with a purchaser introduced by us during the periods of our sole agency or with whom we had negotiations about the property during that period; or with a purchaser introduced by another agent during that period.

**2. MULTIPLE AGENCY**

Commission of     % of the agreed sale price plus VAT.

You will be liable to pay remuneration to us, in addition to any other costs or charges agreed, if at any time unconditional contracts for the sale of the property are exchanged with a purchaser introduced by us (whether directly or indirectly).

**3. JOINT SOLE AGENCY**

Commission of     % of the agreed sale price plus VAT.

You will be liable to pay remuneration to us, in addition to any other costs or charges agreed, if at any time unconditional contracts for the sale of the property are exchanged-

with a purchaser introduced by either of the Joint Sole Agents during the period of our sole agency or with whom we had negotiations about the property during that period;

The commission will be shared between the instructed Joint Sole Agents at their discretion.

Please note that we are obliged to define "Sole Agency" in accordance with the Estate Agents Act 1979 and supplemental Regulations ("the Act")

References to an introduction by Palmer Snell will include both direct and indirect introductions.

**SUB-AGENCY**

If we consider that it may be of assistance in affecting a sale (and providing that you have expressed no prior objection) we may appoint a sub-agent(s), and references to results being achieved through our agency will include the case where results have been achieved in whole or in part through any such sub-agent.

**FEES**

The commission will become due for payment upon exchange of contracts and payable upon completion. VAT at the rate in force at exchange of contracts will be payable on the commission.

The Seller confirms that instruction will be given to a Solicitor, Conveyancer or other legal representative, to pay the commission on the date of completion.

Interest will be charged on any outstanding sum at 5% over the National Westminster Bank PLC base rate and will run from the date of completion, should the account not be paid within 7 days.

**PART EXCHANGE**

In the event of Palmer Snell introducing an applicant who proceeds with a part exchange deal the normal commission will be payable. The commission will be calculated on the aggregate sum of the cash exchange (if any) plus the value of the purchasers part exchanged property.

**EXPENSES**

Any additional marketing costs (such as advertising, brochures photography) and other expenses will be agreed in writing with you and (if applicable) become payable upon invoicing.

Palmer Snell reserve the right to retain or share the benefit of any marketing discounts and commissions.

**OTHER SERVICES**

Palmer Snell offers a wide variety of related services, such as Valuations (Residential, Business and Commercial), Property Auctions, New Homes Sales, Residential Letting and Management, Survey and Professional Services, Commercial Sales and Others. Full details are available upon request.

**MORTGAGE ADVICE**

We will offer all prospective purchasers, without obligation, guidance with their proposed purchase including comprehensive mortgage advice. This advice is also available to sellers prior to marketing their property or alternatively at the time an offer is received from a prospective purchaser.

With nearly 100 Building Societies as well as the High Street Banks all claiming to offer attractive mortgage terms understanding the differences can be daunting. Palmer Snell has solved this problem with a personalised computerised search facility for which no charge is made. Further information available from your local office.

Palmer Snell is a producer to London and Manchester (Agency Financial Services Limited which is a Representative only of the London and Manchester Marketing Group. Members of which are regulated by the Personal Investment Authority and IMRO.

**"FOR SALE" BOARDS**

"For Sale" boards are an extremely important marketing tool. They advertise that the property is FOR SALE twenty-four hours a day, seven days a week; we cannot recommend their use strongly enough.

Under current legislation only one "For Sale" board is permitted outside each property. Contravention of this may result in Palmer Snell and the Seller liable to prosecution by the Local Authority. It is agreed that Palmer Snell should have permission to erect a "For Sale" board and if another agent, with or without your consent, should erect another "For Sale" sign please advise us immediately.

**PERSONAL INTEREST**

Under the Act, we must disclose to you in writing if Palmer Snell or any connected person has a personal interest in your property or is seeking to acquire a beneficial interest in the property, or in the proceeds of a sale of any such interest.

**TERMINATION OF AGREEMENT**

If there is a minimum period stated in the Instruction Agreement. Cancellation of the Agreement may be only on the expiry of 14 days written notice given by either party at the end of this minimum period.

Cancellation of any Agreement where a minimum period is not stated may be made on the expiry of 14 days written notice by either party.

**PROPERTY MISDESCRIPTIONS ACT 1991**

We are obliged to present the details, photographs and advertising in compliance with the above Act. This means that no false or misleading statements may be made and we would seek your understanding and co-operation in achieving this objective.

## SAMPLE SOLE AGENCY AGREEMENT

**INSTRUCTION AGREEMENT**                    Ref. No. [            ]

DATE:................................

CONTACT: ...............................

CODE..............:OFFICE: ..............................

PROPERTY ADDRESS ...............................

.......................................................................

SELLER(S)..............................................

SELLER(S) ADDRESS ...............................

.......................................................................

TEL HOME ................................................TEL WORK ........................

SOLICITOR .........................................................CONTACT ........................

ADDRESS .....................................................................TEL ........................

PRICE to be quoted £ ..............................FREEHOLD/LEASEHOLD*/LENGTH OF LEASE...............

SERVICE CHARGE & GROUND RENT ......................HOW ARE THESE CALCULATED ................

ARE THERE ANY SHARED/COMMUNAL AREAS ...............................

FIXTURES & FITTINGS.................................................................. Negotiable/Included*

CONSTRUCTION OF THE PROPERTY ...............................

ARE THERE ANY GUARANTEES...............................

ARE YOU AWARE OF ANY OF THE FOLLOWING:-

Restrictive covenants                    Yes/No* details ........................

Dispute with neighbours etc.            Yes/No* details ........................

Highway or planning proposals           Yes/No* details ........................

Rights of way, that affect the property  Yes/No* details ........................

Alterations to the property             Yes/No* details ........................

If yes was planning consent & building requirements obtained  Yes/No  details........................

SERVICES CONNECTED    Mains Gas Yes/No      Propane Gas Yes/No      Mains Water Yes/No

Mains Elec Yes/No      Drainage Mains/Private      if private Cesspit/Septic Tank

POSSESSION (When are you likely to be able to complete) ........................

PRESENT MORTGAGE ARRANGEMENTS:-........................

VALUATION ADVICE ...............................

COMMISSION: It is agreed that PALMER SNELL are appointed as SOLE/MULTIPLE AGENTS* for a period of

not less than      weeks from today's date at a commission rate of      % of the agreed selling price plus VAT.

OTHER COMMISSION ARRANGEMENTS:-........................

ADDITIONAL EXPENSES (where applicable)...............................

OTHER AGENTS INSTRUCTED:- ...............................

SELLERS PURCHASE ARRANGEMENTS...............................

**PROPERTY DETAILS**

| PROPERTY DETAILS | | | | | | | APPEARANCE | | AGE | |
|---|---|---|---|---|---|---|---|---|---|---|
| HOUSE | HO | TERRACED | BEDS | No of | | SHARED GARDEN | | VERY GOOD | | PERIOD |
| BUNGALOW | BU | END-TERR | BATH'S | No of | | NO GARDEN | | GOOD | | OLD |
| CHALET | CH | SEMI-DET | | | | SMALL GARDEN | | AVERAGE | | MODERN |
| FLAT | FL | DET-LINK | RECEP | No of | | MEDIUM GARDEN | | POOR | | NON-ESTATE |
| GROUND FLOOR FLAT | GF | DETACHED | GARAGES | No of | | LARGE GARDEN | | STR DEFECT | | SMALL DEV. |
| COTTAGE | CO | | | | | LAND ACREAGE | | RENOVATION | | ESTATE |
| MAISONETTE | MA | OUTBUILDINGS | PARK SPACE No. | | | | | | | |
| BUILDING PLOT | BL | ANNEXE/FLAT | | | | | | | | |
| WARDEN FLAT | WA | | | | | | | | | |
| BARN CONVERSIONS | BN | | AREA CODE OF PROPERTY | [          ] | | | | | | TOWN/RURAL |

CONNECTED PERSON* ........................ FOR SALE BOARD YES/NO* ........................

VIEWING    By Appt. ☐      Key Un Accompanied ☐      Key Accompany ☐

ARRANGEMENTS ........................

I/We* confirm that I/we* have read and agree to Palmer Snell's Standard Terms and Conditions and the information given above is complete and correct. I/We* acknowledge receipt of the Standard Terms and Conditions and of a duplicate of this Instruction Agreement. I/We* warrant that, in the event of the property being held in co-ownership, I/We* have authority to sign this Agreement.

........................                    ........................

Seller                    *Delete where necessary            on behalf of Palmer Snell

# APPENDIX 2

# BLACK HORSE AGENCIES
# HOME REPORT JUNE 1996

**BLACK HORSE AGENCIES REPORT ON AVERAGE TIME TAKING TO SELL A PROPERTY**

*Time taken to sell a property*

Nationally, the time taken from initial instruction to agreeing the sale of a property has remained stable at 21 weeks.

The average time across the country from agreeing a sale to completion has remained at 9 weeks.

**32** WEEKS

**27** WEEKS

**22** WEEKS

**14** WEEKS

**22** WEEKS

**16** WEEKS

HOT SPOTS
- the fastest selling areas

Time taken to sell
(average number of weeks)

| | |
|---|---|
| Reading | 5 |
| Portsmouth | 6 |
| Guildford | 8 |
| Hove | 8 |
| Cambridge | 8 |
| Felixstowe | 9 |
| Gorleston | 9 |
| Letchworth | 9 |
| Luton | 10 |
| Newbury | 10 |

AVERAGE NUMBER
OF WEEKS TO SELL A
PROPERTY

28  27
23
21   14
16

AUGUST 1995 REPORT

30  22
28
17   14
13

FEBRUARY 1996 REPORT

Reproduced by kind permission of Black Horse Agencies

## BLACK HORSE AGENCIES REPORT ON AVERAGE NUMBER OF VIEWERS AND OFFERS PER PROPERTY

*The number of viewers and offers per property*

The number of viewers per property can vary dramatically across the country and can depend on the range of properties available.

*For example, Richmond has 35 viewings - a major factor being that it has many property types from Georgian to Regency, through to Victorian - with no two properties the same. Whereas, some areas have as low as 5 viewings, often due to the properties available being of a similar type and style.*

The average number of different viewers per property has increased to 10 - In February 1996 the average was 9.

### Viewings in the fastest selling areas

(average number of viewers per property)

| | |
|---|---|
| Reading | 9 |
| Portsmouth | 5 |
| Guildford | 6 |
| Hove | 12 |
| Cambridge | 8 |
| Felixstowe | 5 |
| Gorleston | 5 |
| Letchworth | 6 |
| Luton | 7 |
| Newbury | 6 |

AVERAGE NUMBER OF DIFFERENT BUYERS VIEWING A PROPERTY

AUGUST 1995 REPORT

FEBRUARY 1996 REPORT

# APPENDIX 3

# SAMPLE BUILDING SOCIETY REPORT AND VALUATION

## SAMPLE OF A BUILDING SOCIETY REPORT AND VALUATION

**Report and Valuation for Mortgage**

**WOOLWICH**
— B U I L D I N G   S O C I E T Y —

Applicants Copy: This report is for your own information only and your attention is drawn to the notes below.

| Property | Age of proposed security |
|---|---|
|  | Early 1900s |

| Applicant | Occupation: Owner/Tenant/Vacant* | Date |
|---|---|---|
|  | Owner |  |

| Tenure: Freehold/Leasehold/Feudal* | Years unexpired | Home branch |
|---|---|---|
| Leasehold | 82 years |  |

| Ground rent | Fixed/Escalating* | Introducing branch |
|---|---|---|
| £30 pa |  |  |

Description:

**TYPE & AGE:** A self-contained first and second floor maisonette conversion in an early 1900's inner-terraced house on ground and upper floors

**CONSTRUCTION:** Brick construction, front elevation fully colour-washed, under pitched concrete tiled roof. Timber inter-floor.

**ACCOMMODATION:**

**GROUND FLOOR:** Stairs to:-

**FIRST FLOOR:** Hall, living room, kitchen/breakfast room, bathroom/wc.

**SECOND FLOOR:** Landing, 2 attic double bedrooms.

**OUTSIDE:** There is no outside space.

**SERVICES:** All mains services including gas central heating.

**ROADS:** Made up, paved and adopted

Superficial gross floor area
76 sq.m.

Condition, repairs required & general comment:
The property provides spacious two double bedroom accommodation with the benefit of a large living room with coal effect gas fire and a kitchen/breakfast room. All windows except to the living room have been replaced with UPVC double-glazed units. The property has generally been well maintained with the following exceptions:-

1.    The clap boarding to the front dormer is rotting and requires repair/renewal and redecoration.

2.    There is slight vertical cracking over the entrance porch lintel and vertically to either side of the two storey front bay. These appear to be longstanding and non-progressive and the likelihood of further significant movement seems remote.

The property is located in a cul-de-sac of similar age and style properties off Chiswick High Road for local shops and amenities.

*Please delete as required

Subsidence, Heave or Landslip. Please report specifically on any evidence of subsidence, heave or landslip in the property or in the immediate vicinity.
There is no evidence of subsidence, heave or landslip

| Valuation of property | Retention | Reinspection necessary: Yes/No* |
|---|---|---|
| £ 128,500 | £Nil | No |

| Recommended insurance value. Main Property: | Recommended insurance value: Outbuildings |  |
|---|---|---|
| £ 78,000 (maisonette only) | £ | 76 sq.m. |

This is a copy of the report and valuation for mortgage which has been prepared by a Valuer on behalf of the Society as required by Section 13 of the Building Societies Act 1986. It is for the sole purpose of enabling the Society to decide how much should be lent against the security of the property and on what terms. It is based on a limited inspection and a valuer's much less thorough and detailed advice about the property than you need, as prospective owner and occupier of the property. This report is not a structural survey, nor is it a Home Purchase Report, each of which requires a much fuller inspection and gives much more detailed advice about the property suitable for the needs of a prospective owner and occupier, and for which, accordingly, higher fees are charged.

There may be serious defects in the property which are not revealed by this report, or the report may be defective, or there may be omissions or inaccuracies in it which do not matter to the Society but which would matter to you. IT IS IMPORTANT THAT YOU SHOULD NOT RELY IN ANY WAY ON THIS REPORT IN DECIDING WHETHER TO PROCEED WITH THE PURCHASE. The Society strongly recommends that you obtain your own more detailed survey report on the condition and value of the property, based on a fuller inspection, to enable you to assess whether the property is suitable for your purpose both as an investment and a residence. Neither the Society nor the valuer accept any responsibility to you or any other person for the contents or accuracy of the report made to the Society, even if the

valuer has been at fault in his inspection or his report. Nor does the Society or the valuer warrant that the price is reasonable. You should show a copy of this report to your solicitor or other professional advisers, who can explain the limited nature of this report and also the disclaimer of responsibility set out herein. The valuation shown is the valuer's opinion of the current open market value of the property at the date of inspection taking into account its repair and condition and may not be the only valid valuation figure relating to the property.

**NB:    The Woolwich Building Society offers its borrowers a wide choice of more comprehensive valuation and survey reports.**

Reproduced by kind permission of Woolwich Building Society

# APPENDIX 4

# SAMPLE RICS HOME BUYERS' REPORT

## SAMPLE RICS HOME BUYERS' REPORT

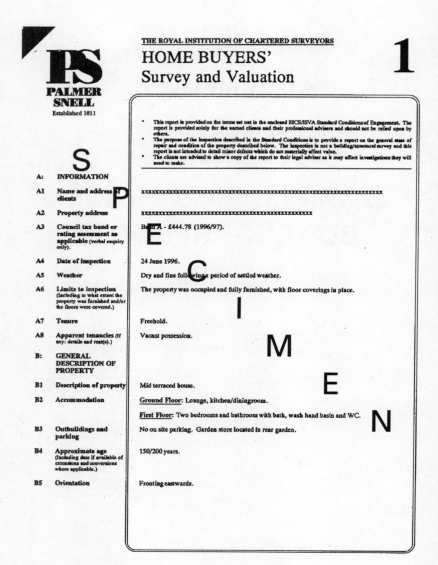

**PS**

**PALMER SNELL**

Established 1811

THE ROYAL INSTITUTION OF CHARTERED SURVEYORS

# HOME BUYERS'
## Survey and Valuation

**1**

S P E C I M E N

* This report is provided on the terms set out in the enclosed RICS/ISVA Standard Conditions of Engagement. The report is provided solely for the named clients and their professional advisers and should not be relied upon by others.
* The purpose of the inspection described in the Standard Conditions is to provide a report on the general state of repair and condition of the property described below. The inspection is not a building/structural survey and this report is not intended to detail minor defects which do not materially affect value.
* The clients are advised to show a copy of the report to their legal adviser as it may affect investigations they will need to make.

**A:**   **INFORMATION**

**A1**   Name and address of clients    xxxxxxxxxxxxxxxxxxxxxxxxxxxxxxxxxxxxxxxxxxxxxxxxxxxxxxxxxxxxxxxxxxxxxxx

**A2**   Property address    xxxxxxxxxxxxxxxxxxxxxxxxxxxxxxxxxxxxxxxxxxxxxxxx

**A3**   Council tax band or rating assessment as applicable (verbal enquiry only).    Band A - £444.78 (1996/97).

**A4**   Date of inspection    24 June 1996.

**A5**   Weather    Dry and fine following a period of settled weather.

**A6**   Limits to inspection (including to what extent the property was furnished and/or the floors were covered.)    The property was occupied and fully furnished, with floor coverings in place.

**A7**   Tenure    Freehold.

**A8**   Apparent tenancies (if any; details and rent(s).)    Vacant possession.

**B:**   **GENERAL DESCRIPTION OF PROPERTY**

**B1**   Description of property    Mid terraced house.

**B2**   Accommodation    <u>Ground Floor</u>: Lounge, kitchen/diningroom.

      <u>First Floor</u>: Two bedrooms and bathroom with bath, wash hand basin and WC.

**B3**   Outbuildings and parking    No on site parking. Garden store located in rear garden.

**B4**   Approximate age (Including date if available of extensions and conversions where applicable.)    150/200 years.

**B5**   Orientation    Fronting eastwards.

**PALMER SNELL**

Established 1811

THE ROYAL INSTITUTION OF CHARTERED SURVEYORS

# HOME BUYERS'
## Survey and Valuation

**2**

**B6    Location and amenities**

The property is located at the southern end of one of the town's principal shopping streets, in an area of mixed quasi-commercial and residential uses. Town centre amenities are within close walking distance.

**B7    Summary of construction.** (Some buildings may not comply with the requirements of today's new buildings, and could include harmful or hazardous materials. This report will include details such materials where their use is apparent from the visual inspection but with certain types of building it may be impossible to confirm the details of construction.)

450mm/500mm thick solid stone and brickwork walls, part rendered and colourwashed, under a pitched slate covered roof.

**C:    EXTERNAL CONDITION**

**C1    Chimney stacks and boiler flues** (including associated flashings, etc.)

There is a single stack, shared with the adjoining property to the north and located over the party wall. The stack is substantial brickwork structure, containing four flues from the subject property, one of which is surmounted by an aluminium cowl. Brickwork and mortar pointing was in maintained and satisfactory condition. Flashings to the base of the stack were formed with leadwork and were cut into the brickwork courses and dressed down to the roof covering satisfactorily.

**C2    Roofs** (including valleys, flashings and soakers.)

Slates to the front roof slope were well bedded and even and in satisfactory condition. Ridge tiles were bedded in mortar and although slightly uneven, were nevertheless in place and adequate. Slates to the rear roof slope were also mainly in place and satisfactory, although the roof slope was slightly uneven. Several slates were split or broken and need to be replaced. Abutment flashings to the adjoining property are formed with leadwork and foil and these were in place and in satisfactory condition at the present time.

**C3    Rainwater goods** (including parapet gutters.)

PVC sectional gutters fitted to front eaves, discharging to shared downpipes in an adjoining curtilage. Gutters were in satisfactory condition. PVC gutters and downpipes to the rear roof eaves were in satisfactory condition.

**C4    Main walls and damp proof course** (The foundations, cavity wall ties or other concealed structural elements have not been exposed for examination and therefore not all defects can be fully diagnosed. The adequacy of sub-floor ventilation is assessed only from the visible exterior surfaces.)

The front elevation was without evidence of weakness or deflection, with openings to masonry believed to be spanned by stone and timber lintels, although these are obscured by render coatings. Render surfaces were uneven and some spalling was apparent, although for the most part they were in maintained and satisfactory condition and do not require significant attention at the present time. The rear elevation was true and straight and is rough cast rendered and colourwashed to finish. There is no evidence of deflection or movement. It should be noted that the external ground level lies 0.3 of a metre above internal floor level.

Party walls to adjoining properties, where viewed from within the subject property, were true and straight and there was no evidence of weakness or deflection.

No inspection of foundations was made as this does not come within the scope of the report and would require the digging of inspection pits, nevertheless, from our inspection of visible

**THE ROYAL INSTITUTION OF CHARTERED SURVEYORS**

# HOME BUYERS'
## Survey and Valuation

**3**

**PALMER SNELL**
Established 1811

structures above the ground we found nothing to suggest inadequacy or insufficiency of foundation support as the dead weights of floors, walls and roofs were adequately carried.

**C5    Windows, doors and joiners**

The front elevation contains a recessed softwood door which is in maintained and satisfactory condition, with portico and apron flashing over. The flashing is worn and will need to be replaced within two years. There is an old bow window to the sitting room and whilst this is serviceable at the present time, consideration will need to be given to its replacement within the next five years as water penetration is likely to occur through joints. The first floor sash window is weathered but in serviceable condition. Timber fascias were satisfactory. Softwood casement windows to the rear elevation were weathered and glazing putty and decorations require attention. Localised rot was present to the sill of the kitchen window and this will need to be replaced. The back door is a double glazed uPVC unit which is in satisfactory condition. Rear fascias were satisfactory.

**C6    External decoration**

Fair order, although redecoration required this summer if timber joinery and render surfaces are to be maintained.

**C7    Garage(s) and outbuildings** (Comment is restricted to important defects, likely to have a material effect on value. Inspection of leisure facilities, etc., is excluded.)

There is no garage. Within the rear garden there is a store building, formed with natural stone and blockwork walls, under a sloping tiled roof. The structure has in part been erected over garden walls and therefore there is likely to be little, if any, by way of foundation structures. Nevertheless, the floor was in maintained and serviceable condition at the present time, although tiles to the caves are flush with the caves boards, with the result that rainwater penetration to the fascias and roof timbers may well occur.

**C8    The site** (Only significant visible defects in boundary fences, walls, retaining walls, paths and drives are reported. Reference to potential hazards such as flooding and tree roots is included where these are readily apparent.)

The property fronts directly onto Holyrood Street and its pavement and there is no front garden. To the rear of the property there is a small enclosed courtyard with patio and concrete finishes which are satisfactory. The rear courtyard is overlooked from the north and south, with the result that there is little privacy afforded.

**C9    Drainage**

(Inspection covers within the boundaries have been lifted where visible and possible (except in the cases of flats and maisonettes). This is to facilitate a visual inspection. The drains have not been tested and it is not possible to comment on hidden areas. Where the drainage systems have not been traced, it is assumed that the drains are connected to the main sewer, or an alternative and acceptable means of disposal.)

A PVC soil vent pipe is located to the rear of the property, which discharges to a chamber located in the garden of the adjoining property to the south. No inspection of the chamber could be made, however, basins and sinks were filled and emptied freely and the drainage system was functioning satisfactorily as far as we can tell, nevertheless, enquiries should be made to establish maintenance liabilities for the system. Connection is believed to be made to the public sewer, although the precise point of connection was not established.

**D:    INTERNAL CONDITION**

(Inspected from floor level only. Furniture, wall hangings, floor coverings, insulation material and stored goods have not been moved. See paragraph D5.)

**D1    Roof spaces** (See paragraph C2. It should be noted that the inspection of the roof space is confined to details of design and basic construction. Individual timbers have not been

The roof is accessed from a hatch on the inner landing. The roof is a purpose built construction, formed with a single hardwood truss with collar and tie, supporting a single hardwood purlin to front and rear roof slopes. The purlins are tusk tenon jointed and that to the rear slope is supported in part by a steel plate to the party wall. The front roof slope has been lifted from its original position and now lies at a new level. This roof is in part supported by a newer purlin at a higher level, which is carried in masonry but also by strutting to the lower purlin. Slate covers and battens were underfelted. The structure is considered to be in serviceable condition and there was no evidence of rainwater penetration. A fire stop wall is formed to the south property

PALMER
SNELL
Established 1811

THE ROYAL INSTITUTION OF CHARTERED SURVEYORS

# HOME BUYERS'
## Survey and Valuation

4

specifically examined for defects although where defects have been observed as part of the general examination, such defects are noted in this report.

abutment with plasterboard, which arrangement is adequate. The party wall to the north is formed with a brickwork structure which incorporates the substantial brickwork flue. Part of the original stack has been taken down but until recently was without adequate support. A steel lintel has been inserted and now is considered to provide adequate support to the free standing areas of masonry. Brickwork to the main flue, however, is badly spalled and brickwork will need to be cut out and repaired, or at the very least, render patched, although in view of the size of the stack and its weight, it is essential that the brickwork contained within its structure does not fracture further, which would allow structural weakness to develop.

**D2    Ceilings**

The ceilings, which were originally lath and plaster, have for the most part been replaced with plasterboard with skim or texture finishes and with plaster coving to some rooms. Timber tongue and groove boarding has been used within the bathroom. Ceilings are all maintained and serviceable.

**D3    Walls and partitions**

Main walls are internally rendered and plastered, with woodchip paper and emulsion finishes, or tiling. Dry linings are fitted to the south wall within the principal bedroom and these are believed to be formed with plasterboard, although with woodchip paper and emulsion finishes. - Wall surfaces were in maintained and satisfactory condition, although removal of existing wall paper finishes may well reveal localised areas of off-key plaster, which will need repair. Partition walls are formed with timber studding and lath and plaster, with woodchip paper and emulsion, or timber studding, clad with plasterboard, with emulsion or tile finishes. Surfaces were maintained and satisfactory. Timber panelling is fitted within the kitchen and sitting room and is in satisfactory condition. Panelling, however, may well obscure dampness contained within the ground floor walls and rot outbreaks may develop over a period of years in view of the presence of some rising dampness (see later in our report).

**D4    Fireplaces, flues and chimney breasts** (It is not possible to indicate the condition of flues or presence of flue liners. No assumption should be made as to the practicability of using the chimneys. It is recommended that any flues should be swept prior to occupation.)

The fireplace in the lounge is inset with a log effect gas fired convector heater. The chimney breasts were supported and the arrangement satisfactory, although regular servicing of the appliance should be carried out. The central heating boiler located in the kitchen is vented through a steel flue pipe to the stack within the roof space.

**D5    Floors** (Only the surface of floors which are not covered have been inspected but accessible corners of any coverings were lifted where possible to identify the nature of the surface beneath.)

Ground floors are of solid construction, formed with cement screed but are overlaid with carpets which prevent a detailed inspection to the surface being carried out. Floors, nevertheless, were level and found to be free from significant dampness, although localised dampness to the floor was found present adjacent to the step from the rear garden. First floors were of suspended timber construction and were level and free from significant weakness, although some bounce was detectible within the principal bedroom. The floors are formed with sawn softwood boards, although again were carpet covered, which prevented a detailed inspection being made.

**D6    Dampness** (A moisture detecting meter has been used in selected accessible positions, without moving furniture, floor coverings, fixtures and fittings, to test for dampness.)

Using our electronic moisture meter we made random tests, which confirmed the presence of localised rising dampness to the main walls. This dampness is however to be expected to an extent in view of the age of the property, although it would be sensible to enquire whether any damp proofing treatments have been carried out in the past, for which guarantees might be available. We do not consider that the dampness present warrants full treatments at the present time, although some nuisance is likely to be caused by the dampness, which will result in localised spalling of plaster and localised wet rot outbreaks occurring in due course.

We found no evidence of penetrating dampness.

**PALMER SNELL**

Established 1811

**D7**    Woodworm, dry rot and other timber defects

Localised wood boring beetle attack was found to be present, however, this is thought largely to be of an historic nature. Enquiries should be made to establish whether any treatments have been carried out, for which guarantees are available, in order to establish the nature or extent of any works. If no such guarantees are available, it would be prudent to arrange for spraying of timber to the whole house prior to purchase.

We found no evidence of dry rot or significant wet rot, although localised wet rot attack is likely to occur to skirtings, in particular, from time to time because of the dampness which we have described in this report.

**D8**    Internal joinery including windows, doors, staircases, built-in fitments and kitchen fittings

The kitchen was fitted with floor standing units and worktops which provide reasonable storage and worktop space. The units are in serviceable condition, although are not of high quality and are worn from use so that minor adjustment to drawer and door fronts is required.

Softwood skirtings and door mouldings throughout were of basic quality but were reasonably maintained. The staircase is a single flight softwood unit, which is in maintained and satisfactory condition.

**D9**    Internal decorations (Furnishings have not been moved to confirm the state of covered or hidden decoration, which may be damaged or faded.)

Fair order, although walls are likely to be marked when fittings and furniture is removed. You will need to budget from the outset for the cost of upgrading the decorations.

**D10**    Cellars and vaults

Not applicable.

**D11**    Thermal insulation

Fibreglass quilting is fitted between the joists within the roof space, although the quilting is to a one inch depth only and additional quilting to bring up to a four/five inch layer is required. The hot water expansion tank within the roof space is fitted with polystyrene panels and would benefit from additional lagging.

**D12**    Services

(No tests have been carried out. Only significant defects and deficiencies readily apparent from a visual inspection are reported. Compliance with regulations and adequacy of design conditions or efficiency can only be assessed as a result of a test and, should you require any further information in this respect, it is essential that you should obtain reports from appropriate specialists before entering into a legal commitment to purchase.)

**D12.1**    Electricity

Mains electricity connected to a service head, credit meters and fuse box located within a cupboard in the lounge. Cabling which was visible was of mainly PVC sheathed type and there was a reasonable provision of 13 amp socket outlets. An electrical circuitry test should however be carried out by a qualified Electrician prior to purchase, when it is likely that recommendations will be given for the replacement of some fittings and localised rewiring.

**D12.2**    Gas

Mains gas connected to a credit meter located within the lounge, where a stop valve was fitted. There was no evidence of leakage.

**D12.3**    Plumbing and heating

Mains water connected with a copper cold and hot water circulating system. There was no evidence of leakage and water pressures were adequate. The hot water boiler which also provides for the central heating is a gas fired unit located in the kitchen. The precise age and service history of the unit is unknown, although we estimate from its physical condition that the boiler is likely to be in the order of 12 to 15 years old and recent servicing has not been carried out. The boiler was functioning satisfactorily when we made our inspection and there was no evidence of leakage.

**PALMER SNELL**
Established 1811

THE ROYAL INSTITUTION OF CHARTERED SURVEYORS

# HOME BUYERS'
## Survey and Valuation

6

Steel panel radiators are fitted throughout the property, with half inch flow and return pipework and individual thermostatic control. The units were free from leakage.

**D12.4 Sanitary fittings**

The bathroom has been refitted with new units within the last few years, which comprise bath, wash hand basin and WC, all in maintained and satisfactory condition.

**D12.5 Other facilities**

Not applicable.

**E:    COMMON PARTS AND SERVICES**

Not applicable.

**F:    FURTHER ADVICE AND VALUATION**

**F1    Road and footpaths**
(including side and/or rear.)

The property fronts an adopted road and footpath.

**F2    Matters apparent from the inspection which should be checked by legal advisers**

**F2.1   Rights of way / easements / servitudes / wayleaves**

Not applicable.

**F2.2   Road agreements**

Not applicable.

**F2.3   In the case of flats, etc., properly formed management company**

Not applicable.

**F2.4   Drains / sewers liability**

To be advised.

**F2.5   Other** (E.g.: significant planning or highway proposals if known. Suspected contravention of building regulations, possibility of enforcement notice and breach of likely planning permission.)

The property is located in a mixed quasi-commercial/residential area, where land uses are likely to change through redevelopment in future years. We are not aware of any significant plans likely to affect the property at the present time.

**F3    Matters that might materially affect value, and any further advice**

**F3.1   In cases of flats, apparent management problems**

Not applicable.

**F3.2   Obvious evidence of serious disrepair / potential hazard to the property**

Damaged brickwork to the stack within the roof space needs to be chopped out and replaced in order to provide adequate support to the structure.

S P E C I M E N

**PALMER SNELL**

Established 1811

**F3.3** Matters not included under F3.1 and F3.2 likely materially to affect the value, and any further advice

Lack of garden amenity and privacy, coupled with the busy road frontage, will deter some purchasers, but equally the property's location close to the centre will provide an opportunity for easy access to the town centre amenities.

**F4** Paragraphs referring to matters regarding the condition/hazards requiring immediate attention (You are advised to obtain estimates of the cost of dealing with any matters referred to here before committing yourself to purchase.)

Paragraph D1 - Repair brickwork to the principal stack.

**F5** Building insurance

**F5.1** Estimated current reinstatement cost in its present form (unless otherwise stated)

(This reinstatement figure must not be confused with the valuation at F6.) (Including any garage and/or outbuildings, site clearance and professional fees, excluding VAT, except on fees.)

£54,000 (fifty four thousand pounds).

**F5.2** Approximate total external floor area of dwelling

72 sq mtrs.

**F6** Open Market Value

(With vacant possession, excluding any development value unless otherwise stated, and excluding the value of carpets, curtains and other sales inducements).

**F6.1** In its existing state

We consider that the proposed purchase price of £33,500 (thirty three thousand, five hundred pounds) reasonably represents the current open market value of the freehold interest with vacant possession, providing there are no onerous covenants or restrictions affecting title.

**F6.2** As if any works referred to at paragraph F4 had been undertaken satisfactorily

£34,000 (thirty four thousand pounds).

**PALMER SNELL**
Established 1811

THE ROYAL INSTITUTION OF CHARTERED SURVEYORS

# HOME BUYERS'
## Survey and Valuation

**8**

S

P

E

This report is provided on the terms set out in the Standard Conditions of Engagement for The Royal Institution of Chartered Surveyors/Incorporated Society of Valuers and Auctioneers Home Buyers' Survey and Valuation. I certify that the subject property has been inspected by me, that I valued the property and prepared this report.

Signature of Surveyor

Name of Surveyor
(and professional qualifications)

On behalf of
(name and address of organisation)

C

PALMER SNELL
16 PRINCES STREET
YEOVIL
SOMERSET
BA20 1EW

Date of report

I

24 JUNE 1996

M

E

N

# APPENDIX 5

# WOOLWICH COST OF MOVING SURVEY (1996)

**WOOLWICH COST OF MOVING SURVEY (1996)**

TWO

# ENGLAND AND WALES

| House Prices | Cost of Selling | | Cost of Buying | |
|---|---|---|---|---|
| **£25,000** | Solicitor | £287 | Solicitor | £296 |
| | Estate Agent (sole agency) | £769 | Land Registry | £40 |
| | | | Searches | £86 |
| | | | Stamp Duty | nil |
| | | | Home Purchase Report | £255 |
| | **TOTAL** | **£1056** | **TOTAL** | **£877** |
| **£50,000** | Solicitor | £310 | Solicitor | £319 |
| | Estate Agent (sole agency) | £1039 | Land Registry | £80 |
| | | | Searches | £86 |
| | | | Stamp Duty | nil |
| | | | Home Purchase Report | £255 |
| | **TOTAL** | **£1349** | **TOTAL** | **£740** |
| **£60,000** | Solicitor | £323 | Solicitor | £333 |
| | Estate Agent (sole agency) | £1224 | Land Registry | £100 |
| | | | Searches | £86 |
| | | | Stamp Duty | nil |
| | | | Home Purchase Report | £315 |
| | **TOTAL** | **£1547** | **TOTAL** | **£834** |
| **£80,000** | Solicitor | £355 | Solicitor | £372 |
| | Estate Agent (sole agency) | £1609 | Land Registry | £140 |
| | | | Searches | £86 |
| | | | Stamp Duty | £800 |
| | | | Home Purchase Report | £330 |
| | **TOTAL** | **£1964** | **TOTAL** | **£1728** |
| **£100,000** | Solicitor | £401 | Solicitor | £421 |
| | Estate Agent (sole agency) | £2009 | Land Registry | £200 |
| | | | Searches | £86 |
| | | | Stamp Duty | £1000 |
| | | | Home Purchase Report | £330 |
| | **TOTAL** | **£2410** | **TOTAL** | **£2037** |
| **£150,000** | Solicitor | £465 | Solicitor | £490 |
| | Estate Agent (sole agency) | £2950 | Land Registry | £230 |
| | | | Searches | £86 |
| | | | Stamp Duty | £1500 |
| | | | Home Purchase Report | £380 |
| | **TOTAL** | **£3415** | **TOTAL** | **£2686** |
| **£200,000** | Solicitor | £549 | Solicitor | £585 |
| | Estate Agent (sole agency) | £3859 | Land Registry | £260 |
| | | | Searches | £86 |
| | | | Stamp Duty | £2000 |
| | | | Home Purchase Report | £430 |
| | **TOTAL** | **£4408** | **TOTAL** | **£3361** |

Figures compiled by the University of Greenwich, School of Land and Construction Management

Reproduced by kind permission of Woolwich Building Society